Microcosmos

THE INVISIBLE WORLD OF INSECTS

Microcosmos

THE INVISIBLE WORLD OF INSECTS

Claude Nuridsany
& Marie Pérennou

Stewart, Tabori & Chang

New York

Wе are alone as we face the animal world, alone in our human element. Sometimes, when our eyes meet these animals, we feel some signs of intimacy. The sensation of a real contact, a mutual recognition, momentarily troubles us. But our minds quickly draw us back to our own world, and the animal, a temporary companion, is lost in an inaccessible land with an unknown language.

The animals around us fill our lives with questions. Each one carries within it the key to the universe. A man and his dog, strolling side by side, are not taking the same walk. They do not smell the same scents, do not leap at the same sound, do not pick up the same trails, do not decipher the same symbols. Nothing in their bodies or minds resonates to the same pitch. Each one walks in a self-created world, a world described by the five senses and interpreted according to a code unique to each.

Animals live in worlds parallel to our own; we can occasionally reach them through fragile passageways. The world of insects is one of the most remote of these non-human worlds. It lies somewhere at the edge of our perception. The path leading to it is strewn with paradoxes and oddities. We must keep our imaginations alert as we enter this world and be prepared to set aside our most firmly held beliefs. Each truth we learn opens a new door to a staggering number of possibilities; each is a tantalizing invitation to push back the limits of human frontiers, to perceive beyond our senses, to understand beyond our reason. The eyes of insects that watch us from another world are like magical mirrors reflecting the strangeness of our own condition.

Through insects we can rediscover the Earth as if it were a strange new planet, ruled by physical forces that lie beyond our understanding. On a human scale, gravity is the ruling force. It is gravity that orients our bodies, dictates the volume of our muscles, guides our movements, and governs the designs of our homes and our machines. All this changes when we look at the scale of insect life. Compared to that of humans, the ratio of their body surface is considerably larger than their volume. In this Lilliputian world, gravity is replaced by surface tension, a force that has little importance in our world.

When an insect falls from a height several hundred times greater than its size, it lands as if on a soft mattress. Air resistance acting on the surface of its body turns it into an aerodynamic parachute. It is because of surface tension that a fly can walk on the ceiling, head down, flouting the laws of gravity. It is also surface tension that allows some insects to perform the prodigious feat of walking on water. The forces at work on the surface of a simple drop of dew are strong enough to capture an insect and hold it prisoner until the sun dries up this liquid tether.

When we started the project for the *Microcosmos* film, we wanted to include every astonishing thing we had seen throughout the years spent watching these inhabitants of the grasses, all the times we had abandoned our dignified postures as bipeds to return to the habits of our childhood, dropping down on all fours to explore a corner of a meadow. The first thing we learned was immobility. Our outsized bodies gradually became concentrated into the tiny area of our eyes. We were nothing more than what lay before us. For as far as the eye could see, there was nothing but wild grasses, a dull blue-green light, a maze of supple stems and long strips of leaves, bunches of flowers over our heads like pagodas, swinging umbrellas, golden clouds of pollen, and flights of feathered seeds. We named this land where we had so often strayed Microcosmos, the little universe.

The whole story about insects cannot be found in entomological treatises. Insects belong to everyone: to children, who have a natural rapport with this hidden world; to poets, artists, and imaginative people everywhere. Insects have always appeared to be living myths. Look at a mantis frozen at the top of a twig. With its extravagant miter and forelegs joined together as if in prayer, it looks like some god of the grasses. Watch the metamorphosis of a mosquito on the surface of the water. The performance of this diaphanous creature emerging from the depths is more spectacular that the chimeric images of early mythologies.

Insects inspire our dreams as much as our rational observation. This is why we conceived of *Microcosmos* as a natural fairy tale, a pantheist hymn to the beauty hidden in these little-known regions. As a counterpoint to the film, we gathered together the most striking elements we met during our interviews with the inhabitants of the grasses. When Marco Polo returned from his adventures he wrote *The Description of the World*; in our own modest way, we created this notebook of miniature marvels on our return from walks through the garden.

An insect in its realm.

6

THE LIFE OF AN INSECT

The insect jerks forward blindly and impassively. Hidden behind its carapace, it clings stubbornly to the top of a piece of grass, desperately lashing the air with its long antennae, as if to capture a scrap of sensation. We feel sorry for this feeble prisoner in its straitjacket, a creature for whom the celebration of the senses seems hopelessly unattainable.

Are insects really the living fortresses, the insensitive monsters that we see through our human eyes? Is the insect condition so remote from our own world? Our observations also depend on our preconceptions. Things are not always what they appear to be—we must explore beneath the carapace of these strange figures; to do so, we must become something like insects ourselves. What do they see through those unmoving round eyes, which look more like radar domes than the windows on the world we see in the eyes of our fellow men?

In the late nineteenth century, Professor Exner decided to use the eye of a glowworm as a photographic lens by substituting light-sensitive film for a retina. He chose for his subject a church bell tower seen through a window. The result was a grainy picture with blurred shapes; the resolution was eighty times less than that of the human eye. Under a magnifying glass, the eye of an insect reveals countless six-sided shapes; these are called facets. Each one is the lens of a simple eye, or *ommatidium*, which also includes a miniature crystalline lens and a retinal cell. The eyesight of an insect depends on the number of ommatidia it has. A glowworm, for example, has 2,500 facets, while a dragonfly has up to 30,000.

For most insects, the size of the facets and the curve of the surface of the eye changes in different areas of the eye. The visual acuity is not the same in every direction. The insect is nearsighted—indeed, everything beyond one meter is blurred—and is also severely astigmatic. An ideal patient for an ophthalmologist! Yet this absurd conclusion only proves that we are still using our human frame of reference. If the insect needs these eyes, which seem to be so defective by our standards, it may be because they can see

Bees slake their thirst on a teasel leaf.

7

things in a different way—things inaccessible to our human eyes that are essential to its own everyday life.

Professor Exner's mediocre photograph does indeed correspond to the insect's retinal image, an image obtained by juxtaposing thousands of simple images provided by the ommatidia. Yet the real question is infinitely more interesting and more revealing: just how does the brain of the insect use this information?

The structure of the compound eye itself is a marvelous compass; it is a precious tool for animals that spend most of their lifetimes in flight. Indeed, each ommatidium is focused on a narrow portion of the area nearby. The image of the sun, for example, will be perceived by only one of the many ommatidium. This characteristic allows the insect to measure, with a high degree of precision, the angle of its flight path in relation to the sun and, if necessary, to memorize this angle so that it can retrace its steps. At night, an insect makes its way by basing its flight path according to an angle that remains constant in relation to the moon.

Faceted eyes serve other useful purposes. They give the insect a very wide field of vision. Dragonflies and horseflies, which have enormous compound eyes, can clearly see objects situated behind them. Insects can also precisely determine distances and detect movement. Indeed, the different elementary lenses see a moving object as a series of separate images—as if in freeze frame, the least movement by an enemy or prey is immediately recorded.

Do insects see colors? The great Austrian naturalist Karl von Frisch spent his life communicating with bees. He was the first person to examine this question from an insect's point of view and to clearly interpret the answers he found. He first placed several different-colored pieces of cardboard on a garden table. He then placed a dish filled with honey-flavored water on the blue cardboard. The bees were soon packed around the food, making multiple trips to the hive and back. He then replaced the blue cardboard with another blue board, moved it to a different place, and removed the bait. A swarm of bees instantly landed on the blue board, seeking the dish. They completely ignored the other boards (the first blue board was replaced with a new one in case any honey had spilled—the bees would have been attracted by the smell). An initial hypothesis would be that the bees do indeed distinguish color; they easily recognized the blue board that held the food they were seeking. But did they in fact recognize it because of the color?

Some humans afflicted with total color blindness detect no colors at all. Yet they can distinguish between squares of different colors—they appear as different levels of gray, depending on the tones (just as the colors in a black-and-white photograph are translated into a gray scale). Is this what happens with bees? Karl von Frisch modified his experiment by placing the blue board with a dish of honey in the middle of a checkerboard that had several different gray squares. He then completely altered the order of the gray squares and removed the bait. The first bees to arrive naturally landed on the only colored square, even though it had the same relative luminosity as one of the gray squares. This time, they clearly recognized the square by its color.

The ophthalmologist Carl von Hess, who opposed von Frisch, was convinced that insects could not discern colors and refuted this experiment. Bees, he declared, could easily have recognized the blue board because of its specific odor—imperceptible to us—created by the colored dye in the paper. Von Frisch modified his demonstration by covering all the boards with a plate of glass. The bees stubbornly insisted on landing on the blue—definitive proof for the one person who was able to understand them.

During one of these crucial experiments, the bees demonstrated a particular enthusiasm: not only did they scrutinize the blue board on which they usually found food, they were also interested in the blue ties and hat ribbons worn by members of the team.

Similar experiments demonstrated that the bees were totally blind to red, a color they could not distinguish from black. They did, however, perceive ultraviolet rays perfectly well, something that is beyond the human range of vision.

Bees therefore see one color more than we do—and one less. Considering the many possible color combinations, we can assume that the color

range of a bee's vision is therefore different from our own. The scarlet corollas of red campion flowers appear black to a bee, who ignores them. The petals of poppies, however, are extremely attractive, because they reflect ultraviolet rays perfectly. Bees can detect a great many nuances among blue and violet flowers, which also reflect ultraviolet light. As for white flowers, a bee sees them either as blue-green or surrounded by a bright, shining ultraviolet halo. The petals of the daisy absorb ultraviolet light—it therefore appears to a bee as blue-green, the complementary color of ultraviolet.

We may object by claiming that a daisy is not blue-green; it is clearly white. But a daisy is neither white, blue-green, nor red—it is a daisy, nothing more. A flower reflects part of the sunlight that strikes it; our brain then interprets these rays as colored impressions. The brain of a bee interprets this same information differently. The flower appears as a beam of multiple rays—we see just what our own eyes allow us to see.

To a bee, flowers in a meadow appear even brighter than they do to us since they stand out against the dull gray-yellow background of grass. The corollas are like gleaming beacons shining in the midst of fog, beckoning the insects on. We would give a great deal to see, if only for a moment, the treasures of a meadow seen through the eyes of a bee.

Many insects—flies, butterflies, and beetles, for example—can distinguish colors, particularly ultraviolet rays. Some butterflies can see red, which bees cannot, and we have observed clear differences in the perception of light rays depending on the species. An interesting fact: all

An ant drinking a drop of dew.

insects that fly from flower to flower are able to distinguish colors. The seductive profusion of shapes and colors displayed by flowers is meant purely for insects (see Chapter Four, The Play of Insect and Flower).

Our eyes can not detect polarized light, which is nonetheless abundant all around us. When light is reflected on the surface of water, a wet sidewalk, a window, or a mirror, it becomes pola-

rized. The light waves, instead of vibrating in an infinite number of directions along their axis of propagation, then vibrate only along a single plane. Physicists are well aware of this phenomenon and analyze it in laboratory experiments.

The insect has no need of instruments—its eye structure allows it to determine accurately the direction of the vibrations of polarized light. The blue of the sky is filled with polarized light. To an insect, the sky is broken up into areas of differing intensity. This monochromatic design

varies with the time of day, and the insect can interpret these changes to perfection. Indeed, this ability considerably reinforces the efficiency of the solar compass. Even if the weather turns cloudy, leaving only a small patch of blue in the sky, an insect can nevertheless easily calculate the position of the sun from the direction of the vibration of polarized light shining from this section of the sky.

One last characteristic of the insect eye leads us directly to the heart of its inner world. When a series of lights is flashed on a screen with increasing frequency, we retain an impression of separate images up to about eighteen images per second. Beyond that frequency, the eye perceives a continuous image. Movies use this visual illusion: we see a film projected at twenty-four images per second as a perfectly continuous image.

This limit of one-eighteenth is also repeated in other senses: air vibrations greater than eighteen per second, for example, are no longer distinct but are heard as a single sound; if something strikes our skin more quickly than eighteen times per second, we no longer feel separate blows on our skin but a constant pressure. Our senses prevent us from distinguishing two separate events that occur at intervals of less than one-eighteenth per second. Experiments have demonstrated that flies and bees are able to distinguish separate movements occurring at more than two-hundred images per second. In a movie theater, a bee would see only an incoherent succession of fixed images separated by long intervals of black.

An insect uses this extraordinary capacity to dissect time: when, for example, it flies at great

A troop of red ants drink around a pool of water.

speeds over its territory, the landscape unrolling under its eyes appears without any blurring. And when you try to flick away a fly with a quick movement of your hand, the insect has ample time to see the approaching danger and change its direction of flight. Our eye sees this sudden arm movement as an unbroken line; the fly, however, dissects it as if it were taking place in slow motion.

A fly's perception of time is expanded in relation to ours. Each second contains ten times as many separate events. And its movements, which always appear to be precipitous to us, are in harmony with this inner time, which contains so many successive impressions. The gestures made by a fly are no faster in terms of the fly's life than our own appear to us.

The bee and the fly perceive many more impressions than we do during the same amount of time. We can therefore assume that a single day would already seem to be much longer and that viewed in their terms, their short life spans of just a few months are not nearly so ephemeral as they seem to be to us.

Insects do not show their moods. But the person who is able to observe how they live day after day can manage, in the long term, to detect some semblance of expression through the position and movements of the antennae. At rest, the insect does not move its antennae very much. But as soon as it settles into a task, it moves these antennae in every possible direction with an extraordinary agility. It may sometimes freeze in the midst of a movement, stand up as tall as it can on its legs, and swing them around slowly in a questioning movement. When an unexpected or worrisome event occurs, the antennae move in a paroxysmal display of activity—the insect cleans and recleans its fragile organs with an obsessional zeal that betrays its intense distress. This attitude of panic occurs frequently when an insect is placed in a situation that is foreign to its usual pattern of life.

Although the importance of antennae in the daily life of an insect has been recognized for a

long time, the exact role of these organs remains mysterious. Even today, we have not fully determined the full extent of their functions.

The antennae provide the insect with a complex information center concerning the external world. These organs are the headquarters for an incredible system of different senses. Yet the sensorial capacities of these minuscule filaments so exceed the imagination that countless experiments would be required before we could document this truth.

A harvest ant transporting a grain of wheat.

The great naturalist Jean-Henri Fabre encountered these limitations when, in the late nineteenth century, he studied the night-flying moth called the giant emperor.

It all started with the unexpected capture of a female emperor moth, which Fabre placed under a bell cage without having any real project in mind for it. That evening, cries from his children brought him quickly from his office into the house, which was invaded with moths as large as bats. Some forty emperor moths had taken over the kitchen and rooms, especially where the female was held in her cage. All these moths had come a great distance because these kinds of moth were rarely seen in the region. What had caused this extraordinary "remote seduction" by the female moth?

After three years of patient study, Fabre had still not deciphered this enigma, but he did pursue his theories as far as he was able, given the knowledge of the time. First of all, he quickly discovered the primordial role of the feathery antennae of the male. When they were removed and the insect was placed far away, the moths were incapable of finding their way to the imprisoned female. Other experiments supported Fabre's hypothesis that the moths were attracted by a scent emitted by the female.

But what an enormous power this "perfumed call" must have. Enclosed in a hatbox placed at the back of a closed closet, the female still attracted an equal throng of suitors. Even more surprising, a massive quantity of naphthalene scattered around the bell cage had no effect whatever on the males' sense of smell. Finally, how was Fabre to explain the moths' having

arrived from both upwind and downwind? How could they have detected a scent that had to travel upwind to reach them? With no further paths to follow, Fabre came up with a theory of a sweet-smelling wave, a sort of scented X-ray that traveled according to its own unique laws.

We now know the reason for this mysterious event. Male night-flying moths have a phenomenal but extremely specialized sense of smell. They can detect only the odor emitted by females of their species and remain totally insensitive to anything else, regardless of the concentration of the scent. No more than a few molecules of this attractive substance needs to strike their antennae for them to set out in search of the emission source, which may be located more than six miles away.

The sense of smell in all insects is located in their antennae. Generally speaking, this sense is more diversified than with night-flying moths. You often see insects tapping the ground with their antennae—which seems to be an odd way to explore smells. Yet in this case, a second sense is being used: the sense of touch. Antennae are both tactile and olfactory organs; they provide

Ringlet butterfly.

12

the insect with a hybrid sense that is totally foreign to humans, a sense that allows them to detect the "shape" of smells. They can distinguish between "round," "square," "hard," and "soft" smells.

When an ant discovers an interesting source of food, it returns to its nest by sweeping its path with a scented dotted line. It touches the ground lightly at regular intervals using the tip of its abdomen, which secretes a scented substance that impregnates the path for several minutes. As soon as another ant crosses this path, it changes its own direction to follow the way to the food. How does it know which way to go to find the food? The spots of scent have a comma shape, which points in the right direction. The path is therefore clearly marked. Far from being an odd quirk of nature, the shape of smells corresponds to an essential practical tool in the everyday life of insects.

Insects that live in groups use smells as a method of communication. When an ant or a bee is in a dangerous situation, special glands secrete an alarm scent, which immediately warns nearby insects. Other scents have a calming effect, while still others trigger aggressive behavior. Ants living in the same colony recognize each other by the overall scent of their bodies, a scent shared by all members of the colony. Once inside the nest, any ant that does not have the authorized scent—which is a highly effective password—is pitilessly driven out.

We often see ants, bees, and wasps standing opposite each other, each one tapping the other's antennae as if involved in an interminable confabulation. It appears that they are using some kind of antennae code. By lightly touching the outside or inside edge, the top, middle, or base of the other insect's antennae, and by using a regular rhythm, the insect can transmit a large number of different signals. After this interchange, he can then offer his own antennae to "listen" to a tapped reply. What do they tell each other? At present, all we know is the antennae sentences that allow wasps and bees to beg some food from a neighbor, along with the two possible replies—assent or refusal. To verify the accuracy of this interpretation, a French researcher studying the problem, Hubert Montagner, decided to construct a minuscule bee-shaped robot fitted with two moving antennae activated by a delicate clockwork mechanism. The movement of the false antennae was programmed to ask for food, and the bees responded by offering the robot a bit of honey!

They probably exchange other kinds of information. Since the antennae language of bees is not the same as for wasps or ants, scientists are confronted with hard-to-solve translation problems.

We are familiar with sight, smell, and touch,

Crickets in the curve of a leaf.

since they play an essential role in our own representation of the world. The sense of "temperature," however, which is also located in the antennae of many insects, is a much more mysterious sense. Our own capacities in this domain remain extremely modest.

This sense is highly developed in bedbugs, and we can well imagine why—using its antennae, the bedbug can detect the heat from the body of its next victim. It can locate the presence of a sleeping person in total darkness. It merely follows the path toward the heat source; the increasing temperature tells it that it is nearing its prey. Mosquitoes use this same sense to spot their food. We humans, as warm-blooded animals, can certainly attest to this ability.

The temperature inside a beehive during the summer months stays at a virtually constant 93° F (to within 0.25° F), since this is the ideal temperature for the development of larvae. When the temperature drops, the bees release heat by vibrating their thoracic muscles without moving their wings. When the temperature rises too high, they fan the overheated air by rapidly beating their wings and by bringing water from the outside to cool off the hive. This efficient thermal control is made possible by the specialized receptors in bee antennae, which can detect variations in temperature to within one-quarter of a degree.

The capacity to detect the presence of water at a distance is also quite common among insects. Once again, this sense is centered in the antennae.

Finally, if these functions are not sufficient, the antennae can also receive sounds. Male mosquitoes have long feathery antennae that vibrate when sound frequencies of around 380 Hz (something like an F sharp on a piano) are transmitted through the air. Their antennae move according to a simple resonance, much the way a crystal chandelier chimes when a given frequency is emitted near it. What does this F sharp represent to a mosquito? The answer is quite simple: it is the note produced by the female mosquito in flight. As soon as it detects this sound, the male sets off in pursuit of his partner. And the male may sometimes land on a cello, provided the musician has played the right note. Fortunately, the male is totally deaf to the vibrations of its own wings—the frequency is too high, so there is no risk of interference.

Mosquito antennae are designed to detect the signal of a given frequency to the exclusion of every other sound. Mosquitoes do not really have a world of sound, no more than the giant emperor moth has an "olfactory world." Yet many insects do have auditory organs, although the location of these organs may seem fairly unconventional to us, to say the least: they are on the legs of grasshoppers and crickets and on the sides of the body in cicadas. They can all hear ultrasonic sounds extremely well. They create songs that have modulated rhythms and notes using their bodies as musical instruments. Their repertoire includes love songs, rivalry songs, triumphal songs, and simple spontaneous songs.

The capacity to hear is not necessarily matched by a capacity to make sound. Certain night-flying moths are totally mute but have hearing organs that are extremely sensitive to ultrasound. This is their best defense used against their primary enemy, the bat. Bats locate their prey by emitting ultrasonic sounds; they then listen to the reflected echo to determine the exact distance between it and the object detected. As soon as the moth perceives this dreaded noise, it lets itself drop suddenly to the ground. This stratagem often saves its life. The sensitivity of an insect is not limited to a few specialized receptors, such as eyes, antennae, and tympana. Its entire body is riddled with minuscule elementary sensorial organs, called *sensilla*, which are all used to communicate with the outside world.

Most often, a sensillum consists of an extremely fine silk that is extraordinarily sensitive to contact, vibration, and air movement. The bristles on grasshoppers and katydids can therefore detect any sound transmitted by the ground, which may be the signal of an approaching enemy.

Flies, butterflies, and bees have countless gustatory sensilla at the ends of their bristly legs. The ability to taste with the tips of its legs is extremely useful to an animal that spends its life gathering pollen from flowers; when it lands, it immediately knows whether its time is well spent in further exploration. The sensitivity of these sugar detectors among certain butterflies is close to one thousand times greater than that of the human tongue.

Yet an insect does not listen only to the external world; it also listens to itself. Physiologists call this *proprioception*, which allows a living creature to be aware of its own location with regard to the external environment. Sensory organs inform the insect about the least movement of its arms and legs, muscle tension, and even the position of various sections of its body in relation to the direction of gravity.

Armor-plated from head to toe, the insect is nonetheless a hypersensitive creature. We may see as mere curiosities of nature the many abilities of an insect, such as the faculty to see polarized light and ultraviolet rays; to extend the length of a moment; to hear ultrasounds; to feel the shape of scents; to measure temperature, humidity, and wind speed; and even to detect the direction of electrical and magnetic fields (a sense recently discovered in certain insects). All these gifts are withheld from us. Yet the insect uses them to construct its own world of perception. Although we live on the same planet, our worlds are radically different. The world limned by our senses has no more reality or accuracy than the realm perceived by insects.

Larva of Empusa egena *at dusk.*

Captions followed by an asterisk are continued on page 154.

Above:
Solitary bees sleeping inside a dead leaf.*

Left:
Spotted asparagus beetle on a stem of asparagus.

17

Above:
Oedemera nobilis in the heart of a wild rose.*

Right:
Suckerlike pads of the emperor moth caterpillar.

Above:
Giant emperor moth.*

Left:
Longhorn beetle on a stem of mullein.

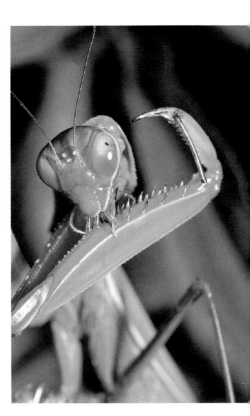

A praying mantis washing up.*

A mantis lies in wait.*

Above:
Ephippiger (wingless grasshopper) on the branch of a juniper tree.*
Right:
Small European fulgorid.

A mayfly at the water's edge.*

A dragonfly at dawn.

Above:
Portrait of a damselfly.*

Left:
Agrion virgo on a papyrus leaf.

Detail of the head of a desert locust.

Common blue butterfly.

An ant carrying a wild lettuce seed.*

Owlfly in a field of grass.

Desert locusts during migration.*

An ant perched on the flowers of a genista.

Above:
Eyes of a gadfly.*

Left:
Owlfly resting during bad weather.

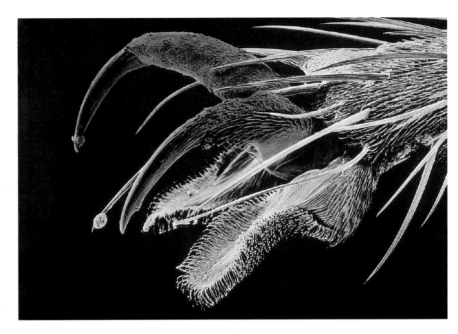

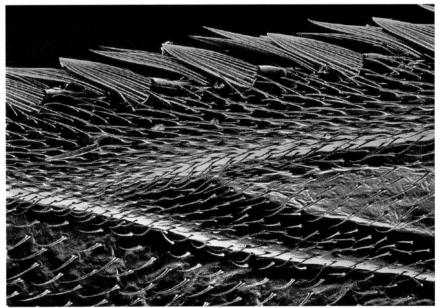

Details of the legs and wing of a fly.*

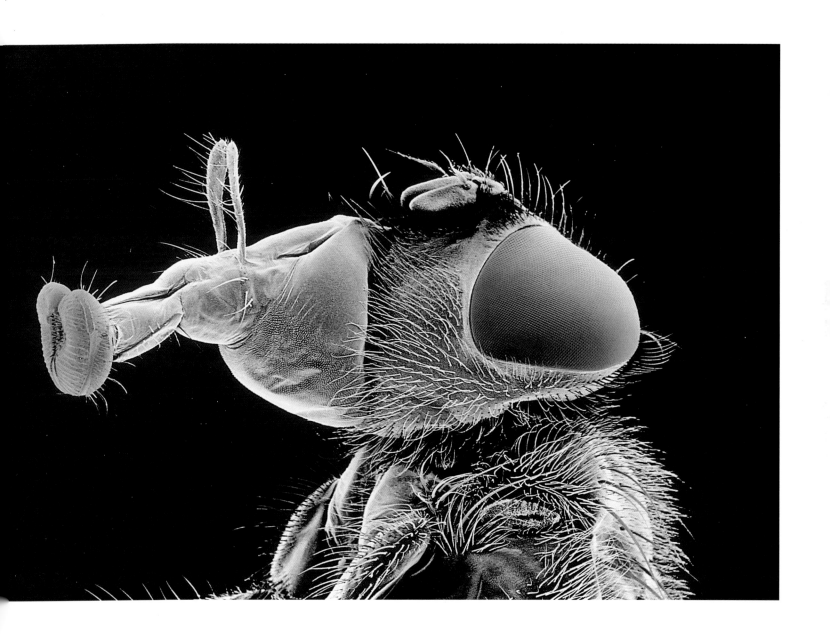

Head of a fly.*

A dragonfly on his watchtower.

A DOUBLE LIFE

Who has not dreamed of having several lives or living in several different skins, each one adding a new experience of the world to the one that went before? This longing is gratified only during sleep, the dark side of life, when metamorphoses of any kind become possible.

Myths and religions have long reflected fears and desires. It is not surprising that many express belief in the possibility of successive lives. According to the Hindu religion, the soul goes through a dizzying merry-go-round of countless rebirths and may return as a man, a plant, an animal, or even a god.

There is no smoke without fire, nor is there myth without some basis in the real world. The *Upanishads*—sacred Hindu texts written some 2,700 years ago—discuss the transmigration of souls, using as an example the metamorphosis of the caterpillar as a chrysalis into a butterfly and, in so doing, identifying the natural source of this fundamental myth. Also revealing is the word *psyche*, which in Greek means both "soul" and "butterfly." The image of the butterfly emerging from its chrysalis has often been used to reflect the mythical image of the soul freeing itself from the body.

Mankind's persistent dream has actually been the everyday reality of countless animals for millions of years. For example, just as in *Through the Looking-Glass*, we can consult a mere caterpillar and see where its unique destiny—which has so captivated human imagination—will lead. The European cabbage butterfly, a small yellow butterfly with black spots, is a common sight; among lepidopterists, it is the equivalent of the sparrow. We have often raised them ourselves and never tire of watching the fascinating theatrical show of their existence.

The adventure starts under a cabbage leaf, where you can sometimes discover up to one hundred small, golden-yellow beads. These are the cabbage butterfly eggs, a single batch of which is often sufficient for a prosperous crop. Under a magnifying glass, the eggs appear to have a delicate lacelike surface. The fine natural handiwork decorating the surface of the cabbage leaves actually indicates a network of small time

Naiad, the aquatic larva of a dragonfly.

bombs—they signify the imminent ruin of a significant number of cabbages.

If placed in a bottle filled with water, the "decorated" leaf stays perfectly fresh. After several days, the golden beads turn a grayish color. And suddenly, dozens of small black heads appear, eating their way through the wall that imprisons them. Using their mandibles as can openers, the newborn caterpillars quickly move toward freedom by decapitating the eggs.

The first thing a caterpillar does is to eat—and it continues to eat incessantly throughout its entire existence. It first consumes the entire egg it has just left behind, then proceeds to devour the plant supporting all the eggs. A gaping hole soon appears in the leaf, which grows visibly larger under the onslaught of a row of starving mouths.

The pudgy, well-fed appearance of the caterpillar reflects its insatiable nature. At this stage, it is basically an intestine disguised as an animal, with a few extra appendages—three sets of clawlike legs and five sets of abdominal suckerlike pads that propel it toward an unceasing supply of food. In just a few hours, the cabbage leaf is nothing more than a pathetic piece of lacework. Only ribs that are slightly too large or too tough for the young mandibles are spared.

The newborns, however, sport a resplendent green coat because the contents of their well-filled digestive tubes appear through the still translucent tegument. A noise like incessant rain soon starts—this is the sound of the excrement of countless caterpillars falling to the ground.

This profusion of food is put to good use by the young caterpillar. Like all insects, it is covered with a fairly inelastic membrane of chitin; as it grows, it must periodically create a new cuticle or exoskeleton. Its head contains sclerotin—the strong substance that reinforces the carapace of insects, making it as rigid as a mask. After four days of feasting, the caterpillar comes to rest on a leaf in a state of complete prostration. It then replaces the cuticle that has become too small with another, slightly larger one, more suited to its size and age. By contracting its abdominal muscles violently, the caterpillar forces the blood to flow toward its thorax, which splits open the cuticle. It then extricates itself from its cast-off clothing through this tear, while the carapace of its head pops out intact like a bottle top. Gulping down great gasps of air that rapidly inflate its body, it grows to fit the larger-size shell before the new cuticle can harden in the air.

This sudden change in size, which occurs as if by magic, is the final outcome of a long period of preparation. A new, larger cuticle is first developed under the older skin like a lining; it remains folded up like an accordion. Between the two cuticles, glands secrete a liquid filled with enzymes, which gradually eats through the older cuticle from the inside out. The products of this digestive process are used by the new cuticle, which absorbs them as the older one thins out. At the end of the process, the caterpillar merely expands its breastplate to split the fragile external skin. At this point, the insect merely has to toss off its old rags and smooth out its new clothes.

During the molting process, the caterpillar undergoes changes of more than its outer skin: the intestinal and tracheal walls, or respiratory channels, are also renewed at this time. This is because the same cuticle that covers the body of the caterpillar also sheathes the inside of the intestines and tracheae. It is therefore logical that when the caterpillar changes its outer coat, it also changes it pockets.

The caterpillar eats twice its body weight in leaves every day, attaining its final size after molting four times. After three weeks, the worm, small and fragile at birth, has reached a highly respectable size. The gluttonous diet has resulted in a spectacular weight gain; indeed, the caterpillar multiplies its initial weight by several thousand times. In its last stage, the caterpillar finally interrupts its obsessional activity; it loses interest in food and wanders to the right and left, lifting itself up on its legs as it swings its head around, as if consumed with distress. This ceaseless dithering means that a serious decision must be made. Finally, the animal takes up residence on the thick rib of a leaf.

It first constructs a silk cushion made of interwoven threads secreted by its mouth and attaches itself to this cushion with its last set of suction pads. It then strengthens its position by weaving a thick belt that holds the thorax tightly against the leaf. This is exactly how a mountain climber would secure himself to the edge of a ledge in preparation for the night. But for the caterpillar, this meticulous ritual is the prelude to a prodigious transformation. Its life as a caterpillar ends with these final gestures.

Once tied in, the caterpillar becomes stiff and starts to shrivel up. Its life seems to be seeping away. If you were to touch it, it wouldn't react—its muscles could no longer respond.

One day later, the skin of the caterpillar just behind the head splits open to reveal a strange

oblong sarcophagus: this is the chrysalis. The old cuticle slides down, pushed off by violent, wavelike movements. Two weeks of immobility follow. The etymology of the Greek word *chrysalis* is "golden age." It is the age of gestation and diffuse awareness, during which the future being is reformed within the tranquillity of a protective shell. What is happening within this stubbornly closed box? What secrets of transformation does

it harbor? Whoever attempts to force open the gate of this fragile fortress would encounter a disappointing, formless mass. The ongoing changes are so intense that they require a total remake of the old organism, and this task occurs through a process of self-digestion. This operation requires a great deal of energy, which is provided by the comfortable reserves of fat accumulated by the devouring caterpillar.

The butterfly about to be born does not leave completely behind the caterpillar organism that

Four seconds in the metamorphosis of a fly.

gave it its former life. Only the highly specialized larval structures, such as the silk-producing glands, are slated for total disintegration. Other organs—including muscles and the circulatory system—are merely remodeled. Yet all the specific attributes of the butterfly—wings, proboscis, antennae, compound eyes, and reproductive organs—must be formed. How can they be created from the chaos within the chrysalis?

Actually, at birth the caterpillar already contains shreds of the butterfly it will become. These are small patches of embryonic cells disseminated throughout its body, which are called imaginal buds (the word imaginal is derived from the word *imago*, a general term designating the mature adult insect). The development of these imaginal disks is temporarily blocked during the caterpillar stage. In the chrysalis, the cellular islands suddenly awaken. The cells divide at a frenetic pace, lose their embryonic characteristics, and begin to differentiate. These tiny, disparate puzzle pieces finally come together to create the butterfly.

About twelve days have gone by. The yellow-green wall of the chrysalis starts to turn brown, then translucent, revealing a few recognizable shapes: a compound eye, an antenna, and most dramatic of all, the folded colored wings that resemble a short cape. The secret is now half revealed. After a few more hours, two suture lines suddenly break open along the back and slowly separate. Two hemispherical eyes open up on a new world.

The winged creature contorts its body to free itself of its sheath. It uses its newly freed legs to liberate the rest of the body. The wings are still nothing more than paltry, crumpled-up stumps. The butterfly forces blood into the veins of the wings by a sudden, contracting movement of its body, which after a few minutes allows them to unfold. After this reincarnation, the butterfly flaps its wings two or three times as a test, then is ready to launch into its new existence. The only memory of its prior lifetime is a large drop of brownish liquid called the meconium (this is also the term used for the first bowel movements of a human newborn), which contains the excretion products and degenerated remains of the larval intestine. This is expelled through its anus before the first flight. The famous "rain of blood," long ago mentioned in legends of the countryside, results from a massive rebirth of butterflies in a single place—the ground is then covered with an unusual scarlet-colored dew.

After it has cast off its cocoon, the butterfly enters its second life. The chrysalis does not move or eat. It is a sheltered envelope, a sort of super-egg, in which a new embryonic development occurs. In the eighteenth century, the Swedish naturalist Linné suggested the name *larva* (which means "mask" in Latin) for the immature form of an insect and *imago* (image) for its adult form. During metamorphosis, the insect throws off its mask to uncover its true face, to finally reveal the true "image" of its species. Even today, descriptions of insects still refer to the characteristics of the adult, or *imago*.

A good sense of observation is all you need to watch the process linking two such seemingly different creatures as the caterpillar and the butterfly. Understanding the preordained sequence of this sudden remodeling of an organism is something else altogether, requiring all the resources available to modern biologists. Yet the mysteries surrounding these prodigies of living matter are far from being solved.

If you were to tie a thread around the middle of a caterpillar when it was in its final stage, or instar, you would observe that the two sections of the animal evolve quite differently. The front part would transform into a chrysalis as usual, while the tail end would stubbornly remain a caterpillar, eventually degenerating. This experiment was repeated using chrysalises. The chrysalises from a first group were cut in the middle and the cut of each section was capped with a plastic cover. A second group was cut in the same way, but the two halves were connected by a thin plastic tube. After several weeks, only the front halves of the chrysalises in the first group had metamorphosed. All the chrysalises in the second group, however, were transformed and, aside from the strange transparent corset separating their bodies in two, the resulting butterflies were normal.

These results suggest that metamorphosis depends on factors contained in the front part of the body. Scientists finally identified the source of this mysterious elixir—a minute gland located in the front ventral section of the thorax. The secretion from this gland was called the molting hormone, or ecdysone. Unfortunately, one of the characteristics of hormones is that only very weak doses are required to be effective. To extract 25 milligrams of pure ecdysone, close to half a ton of silkworm-moth chrysalises were sacrificed!

A second hormone is also involved—this is the juvenile hormone, produced by the corpus allatum situated at the rear of the brain. It modulates

the action of the molting hormone. The role of ecdysone is to trigger the molt. Metamorphosis does occur during a molt if a certain quantity of juvenile hormone is in the blood; this is what happens during the growth period of the caterpillar. When the juvenile hormone secretion drops below a certain level, the molt results in a chrysalis. Finally, when the secretion of the juvenile hormone stops, the molt produces a butterfly.

We have therefore been able to obtain dwarf butterflies by removing the corpus allatum from young caterpillars. These then transform into miniature chrysalises long before they normally would do so. The opposite result has also been achieved—implanting corpus allatum in a caterpillar that has reached its final instar triggers several supernumerary larval molts, which results in a giant chrysalis.

The unfortunate halves of the chrysalises that were unable to metamorphose completed the transformation process only after they received implants of thoracic glands, which produce ecdysone. Once strong female butterfly abdomens were obtained, the females were able to attract male butterflies by emitting the proper scent and eventually laid a good batch of eggs.

For the time being, the ultimate control of these process seems to be housed in the brain of the insect. Scientists have discovered cellular

areas that stimulate the activity of the thoracic gland, while others excite or inhibit the production of the juvenile hormone.

This is undoubtedly the ultimate surprise of these experiments. Why should we be surprised that the tumultuous life transformation of the insect is controlled by a maze of subtle mechanisms? The scientific process often answers questions by posing many more. How can we explain, for example, that simple chemical substances such as hormones can so radically alter the form of a

living creature? We now have several elements to help answer this question.

The organization of every living being and its structures and functions are managed at a microscopic level by genes, which are the building blocks of heredity and are present in the chromosomes of every cell. Chromosomes can be compared to genetic libraries, in which the genes function as assembly and maintenance manuals allowing the organism to construct itself and operate optimally. We can therefore imagine that when a caterpillar is born it possesses two genetic assembly programs: one caterpillar program, which provides the intial set of instructions, and a butterfly program, which is temporarily out of service. Depending on the stage of growth, hormones operate to block or stimulate these two groups of genes.

Many experiments performed on larvae of midges (which produce an insect similar to the mosquito in the adult stage) seem to confirm this hypothesis. This larva has giant chromosomes in its salivary glands that offer the advantage of visibility under a microscope. When ecdysone is injected, very clear bulges appear on specific sections of these chromosomes. This is immediately followed by the first changes that prefigure metamorphosis. The hormone therefore seems to act by stimulating certain chromosomal segments, or batches of specific genes; these trigger the start of the new program.

Butterflies are not the only creatures with this metamorphic ability; indeed, most insects have the transformative power of Proteus. A small number of them transform gradually—in certain larvae, several elements reveal the appearance of the future adult, particularly in the small, roughly formed wings that become more apparent as growth proceeds. During the last molt, the wings suddenly attain their definitive size, while the rest of the body may also undergo major transformations. These insects are called hemimetabolic, which indicates their incomplete metamorphosis. This is the case with dragonflies, crickets, grasshoppers, praying mantises and cicadas.

Finally, there are extremely primitive, wingless insects that do not transform during their first growth period. These include the silverfish, which are common in damp areas of houses, or the minute collembola, or springtails, tiny insects that live in the soil. These are ametabolic.

The evolution of insects resulted in the division of their lives into two distinct periods. The first insects were ametabolic—the monotony of their lives was broken only by simple growth molts. Then some 400 million years ago, new groups appeared—cockroaches, dragonflies, and mantises—that began to have elements of a dual life. From that time on, the split between the larva and the imago was complete. The consequence of this dual genetic program—in which one set of genes controls the larval form while another controls the adult form—was that two phases of the same insect species could evolve independently from one another in geological time, as if they were two different animals! As the dissimilarity between the larva and the adult increased, a simple imaginal molt—a metamorphosis that ended the larval period—was no longer sufficient to ensure the passage from one to another. To breach this gap, an intermediary

step had to take place so that the organism could have enough time to restructure itself. This stage is called the chrysalis for butterflies and the pupa for flies.

The enormous energy reserves of the pupa mean that the insect does not have to worry about feeding itself. Furthermore, the rigid shell, which does not attract predators, shelters it. The pupal stage made transformation possible from

the white worm to the spinner, the maggot to the fly, and the caterpillar to the butterfly.

After a life as a lowly larva, condemned to constantly eating, followed by a somnolent pupal life, the winged insect is free to conquer the skies. Often, however, it barely has time to taste the freedom of flight before its life is over. The adult insect consumes itself in an excess of activity, precipitated by the necessity of procreation. Indeed, its existence rarely lasts longer than a brush fire.

Metamorphosis
of a desert locust.*

1

2

3

4

5

6

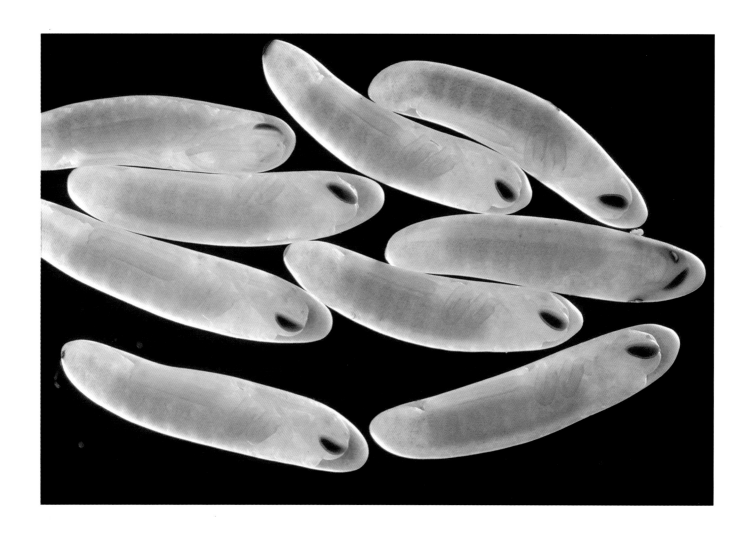

Above:
Desert locust eggs.
Right:
Larval remains of a cricket just after metamorphosis.

50

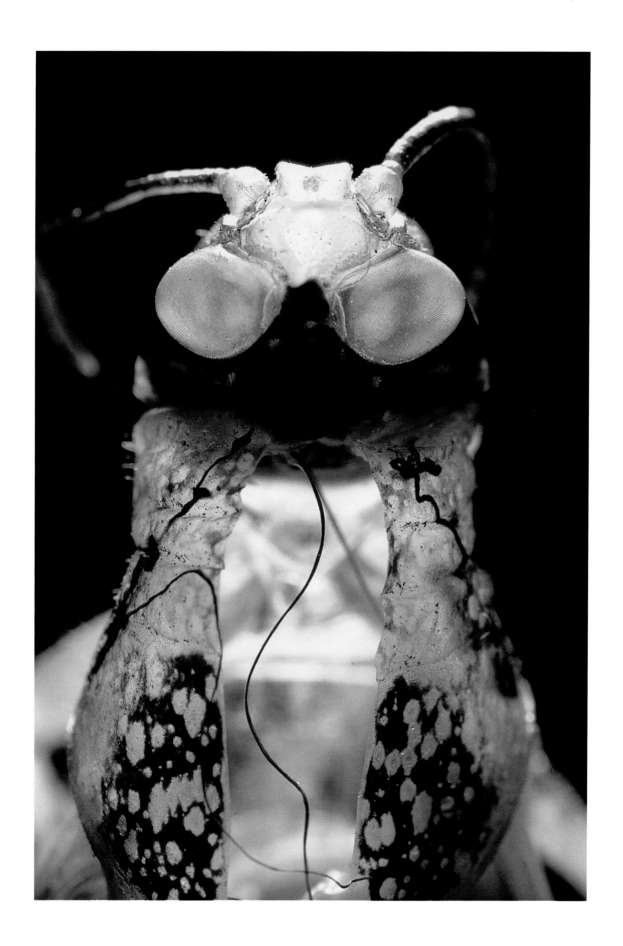

Metamorphosis of a ladybug.

3

4

6

53

Wasp queen on her nest.*

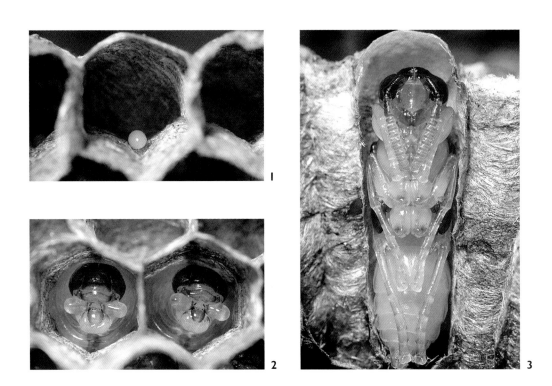

4

5

Birth of a worker bee as it emerges from its cell.*

55

Above:
Damselflies laying eggs.*

Left:
Damselflies mating.*

Green lacewing eggs hanging from a stem of dill.

A dragonfly near its molt, just after metamorphosis.

Metamorphosis of a fly.*

Fruit fly on a stem of field grass.

Chrysalis of the sphinx moth.

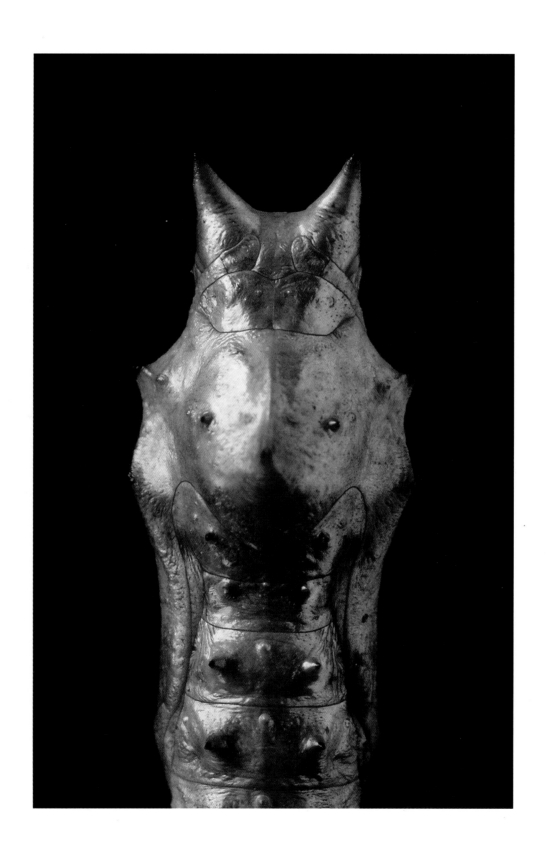

Chrysalis of the peacock butterfly.

A bumblebee (seen from the back) warming up its wings before takeoff.

INSECT INVENTIONS

Watching flies in flight is not considered an enriching experience. But what about the thrill of seeing the aerial acrobatics performed by pilots during air shows?

Just once, take the time to observe the erratic trajectory of a fly. What airplane could turn so sharply, stop instantly in the middle of a high-speed acceleration to remain in stationary flight, fly backward, or land in an instant without braking or sliding, even when upside down?

The conquest of the sky is not a human adventure—it belongs to the insect realm.

Insects were the first inhabitants on Earth to solve the difficult problem of flight. Reptiles (such as the pterodactyl in the Jurassic period) later made a few awkward attempts, followed by birds, a successful evolutionary step that has endured to this day. Finally, mammals (bats) were able to launch themselves skyward.

Oddly enough, it was the first insects that were the most astute in confronting this challenge. Their solution to the problem of flight was infinitely more elegant than all others developed later by vertebrates.

The insect is the only flying animal that did not lose other ambulatory organs when it acquired wings. Birds and bats can fly only because their front limbs were transformed into propulsion organs, which were no longer available for walking.

The insect is an example of a completely successful hybrid creature—it can crawl on the earth as well as fly. It combines in a single body the attributes of these two contradictory modes, with six subtly articulated slender legs for the earth and two sets of diaphanous wings for the sky.

Insects wings are so thin that they don't even seem to be made of living material. Everything contributes to an ideal compromise between lightness and strength. Two thin, transparent membranes stretched between narrow rigid veins create a strong and flexible surface. They are similar to the ribs of balsa-wood model airplanes covered with rice paper. This lightweight flying surface is perfectly designed to

Mole cricket.

stir up air. Its shape protects it from rips and tears. The front or leading edge withstands the greatest stress during flight; it is reinforced by a network of large veins that diminish very quickly from the edge so that there is no unnecessary weight on the rest of the wing. The opposite or following edge is as thin as a piece of tissue paper.

Where, then, are the muscles that control these wings? This is one of the best things about the flight apparatus of an insect—the power-producing function is contained entirely within the thorax. The wings are not weighted down by a single extra gram of muscle tissue, which creates the smallest possible inertial force. Some mosquitoes can beat their wings at speeds of 1,000 times per second. The hummingbird, the record-holder among birds, can beat its wings only 50 times a second; muscles, bones, and feathers obviously can not be added with impunity.

But let's return to the heroic era of early flight, some 350 million years ago. At that time, the sky belonged to a great dragonfly, the Meganuera, which measured close to 30 inches (75 centimeters) across. Aside from their size, dragonflies today resemble these giants almost exactly. This prototype must have had an extremely good design to produce such a long lineage.

Yet the delicate trajectory of dragonflies over water is really an archeological display of flight. Compared to those of other insects, the techniques used by dragonflies to overcome the tyranny of gravity seem outdated.

The first questionable point in their flight technique is that their wings do not beat in unison, which is a rather offhanded approach to the laws of aerodynamics. Indeed, the trajectories described by the two sets of wings result from opposing movements (one set of wings moves up while the other moves down). The multiple interactions occurring between these two tandem drive systems—air flow and turbulence, for example—reduce the efficiency of the flight. Dragonflies have another archaic characteristic: the "drive unit" and the "transmission" organs. The dragonfly wing is driven by a pair of large antagonistic muscles (the alary muscles of dragonflies account for one-quarter of their total body weight); the base of these muscles is connected directly to the thorax on either side of the joint. This "direct drive" system controlling the muscular energy of the wings does not allow them to beat very quickly. With only 20 to 30 beats per second, the dragonfly beats its wings even more slowly than a hummingbird.

Despite these rather theoretical drawbacks, the dragonfly is nevertheless a remarkably fast, flexible, and accurate flyer. It is even one of the fastest insects in flight and can reach speeds of up to 30 mph (50 kph).

What gives a dragonfly mastery over his realm, the pond, is a subtle "flight control" system possessed by only the dragonfly and the fly, which is the most evolved six-legged flying machine. The dragonfly operates according to an inertial-guidance system. It's head can move much more freely than its thorax. When the insect is in flight, the head remains in a horizontal position, regardless of the position of the

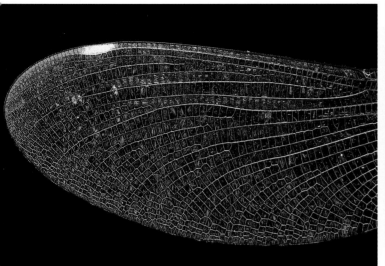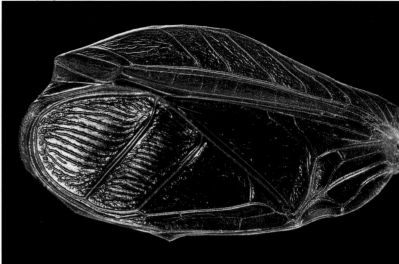

body and wings. The head therefore acts as an inertial-guidance device, much like a gyroscope. It constantly provides the animal with its exact position in relation to a horizontal line. When the body moves away from its horizontal reference, multiple sensor bristles implanted between the head and the thorax are stimulated by the relative shift of these two portions of the body, and the insect changes its flight accordingly.

All the more evolved insects have given up the direct-drive system used by dragonflies. Their wings are controlled by muscles that are no longer part of the actual wing structure but are connected to the inner wall of the thorax. A first group of vertical muscles flattens the thorax from top to bottom, which causes an upward wing stroke. This stimulates the long muscles controlling the downward wing movement. This alternating effort by two groups of antagonistic muscles is independent of nerve impulses and can occur at very high speeds. (In dragonflies, however, the direct-drive muscles must receive a nerve impulse before they can contract the muscle that controls the wing movement.) This remarkable automatic system depends on the elasticity of the thorax. This

unique technique allows incredibly fast wing speeds: 200 beats per second for the common housefly, 300 for the bee, and 600 to 1,000 for the mosquito!

Primitive insects, such as the mantis, cricket, and grasshopper, are still propelled by asynchronous wing movements and the direct-drive technique that evolved with the dragonfly. Yet they added a few useful improvements to the original design. At rest, their wings can be brought along the length of their bodies, so that these do not interfere with walking. The front wings are thicker and cover the membranous rear wings with a protective shield.

Beetles took this secondary evolution of the first pair of wings even further; they were transformed into armorplates, or elytron. These rear wings serve almost no active purpose in flight since the driving force is essentially provided by the front wings.

Beetles seem to have spent more evolutionary energy on walking than on flying. Look at their heavy, squat shape and their extreme reluctance to unfold their wings—these creatures are obviously stubbornly attached to the ground. Butterflies, bees, flies, and mosquitoes, on the other hand, have more fully exploited the

Detail of a dragonfly wing and a cricket wing.

aerial option, by taking on the problem of flight from another viewpoint.

Looking back over the development of aviation, biplanes and triplanes have disappeared, leaving only monoplanes. In their own way, insects tell a similar story. The independent beating of the dragonfly's double set of wings— a uselessly complicated and fragile system— was replaced in more evolved insects by a single, more efficient, and stronger wing system. The two sets of wings do in fact still exist, but a different coupling system makes the rear wings totally dependent on the front wings. Each set of two wings thus forms a single functional unit. Flies simplified the wing structure even further. By definition, insects have two sets of wings, yet flies are unorthodox, since it is an exaggeration to count the two tiny hindwings, or halteres, hidden behind the membranous wings as true wings. Yet they are indeed modified wings. These club-shaped halteres vibrate at the same time as the wings. They are covered with sensory hairs and are essential to a fly's flight control. Whenever the insect changes direction, however slightly, inertia creates pressure at the base of the halteres, which results in a discharge of nerve impulses.

The fly interprets these coded messages and adjusts its flight according to this sensory information. If these halteres are removed, the fly will crash straight to the ground.

An airplane pilot constantly consults his instrument panel; an insect does much the same thing by integrating all the various data provided by its sensory receptors—eyes, halteres, and face and wing bristles—as it moves through the air. Even before it takes off, a special sense informs the insect whether the atmospheric conditions are satisfactory for flight. The fly also has wind-speed detectors located at the base of its antennae. If the wind is blowing harder than 7 1/2 feet per second, the fly will not take off.

These organs also function as speedometers during flight. The faster the insect flies, the more its antennae curve backward—in other words, the receptors receive more stimulation. A fly will accelerate or decelerate depending on the angle of its antennae. Researchers have performed experiments by immobilizing a fly's antennae in a given position. When the fly is released, it flies more slowly as the curve of its antennae is increased; because it believes it is flying faster, the fly slows down.

Finally, insects have more than exceptional flying skills; they also have phenomenal endurance in flight. Migratory butterflies travel considerable distances and often fly nonstop from one continent to another and across oceans in order to reach their summer destination. Every spring, the painted lady butterfly flies close to 3,000 miles (5,000 kilometers) from Newfoundland to Mexico. The desert

Grasping foreleg of a praying mantis.

locust can fly for twenty hours at a cruising speed of 10 mph (16 kph).

All these long-distance flyers use their fat reserves as fuel, while flies and bees—which never travel very long distances—draw their energy from sugars. Migratory insects are more energy efficient, since fats "burn" at a much slower rate than sugars. A bee laden down with nectar will run out of fuel and have to stop after about four miles (six kilometers).

Insects can perform these muscular feats because of their unique respiratory system: the tracheal system. Oxygen is taken in from the air through multiple orifices, called spiracles, located along its sides. It is then distributed throughout the organism through a system of narrow tubes, the tracheae, which branch and rebranch down to a cellular level. Oxygen is therefore renewed very rapidly. But this "direct" respiration—which occurs without lungs or hemoglobin—is possible only in small organisms.

The insect is a perfect flying machine: if it were larger, it could not retain all the sophisticated mechanisms that allow its aerial exploits. Mastery in the art of flight does not occur without some concessions. Over hundreds of millions of years of evolution, the insect has developed its efficient flight capability by remaining small. The giant insects in science-fiction films—a modern version of the bogeyman—will never take over anything but our imaginations.

Insects are the pioneers of flight. They also have another unique skill, that of "water skating." The gerris, commonly known as a water strider or skater, is actually a bug, not a spider.

It is the champion of this quasi-miraculous discipline and can zigzag across a pond like a tiny water-skier. When it suddenly stops, it doesn't fall into the water but remains upright on its threadlike legs as if it were standing on a piece of glass.

The water strider developed something even more unique than water-skiing—it uses its short front legs to capture its prey, its middle legs to drive itself forward (a single leap can propel the water strider close to one yard), and its back legs as rudders.

In the miniature world of insects, a water strider sees the surface of a pond much differently than we do. Molecules in a liquid mutually attract each other in all directions. But on the surface, this molecular attraction is essentially directed toward the inside of the liquid—the molecules are therefore better organized and have a greater cohesion. They are drawn together, forming a kind of elastic mesh. The surface also tends to contract to the smallest possible surface area, much like plastic wrap. Scientists call this phenomenon surface tension.

This molecular skin covers the surface of standing water like a flexible mirror; objects interact with this film in different ways. If the object on the surface is absorbent, or what physicists call hydrophilic, the skin moves upward toward the object and splits open—and the object is engulfed in an instant. However, if the object is non-absorbent, or hydrophobic, the skin hollows out but remains intact (provided the object is not too heavy).

Under a microscope, a water strider appears to be sheathed in a felt coating consisting of thousands of hairs coated with a waxy, water-repellent secretion. One final design touch: claws, by nature absorbent, are usually located at the ends of the legs, but in these insects they are retracted into a recessed position. They do not, therefore, interfere with the efficiency of the hairs by breaking the surface of the water.

The feat of the water strider lies forever beyond our reach. Professor Baudin, a specialist in aquatic insects, calculated that if we wanted to copy the water strider, we would

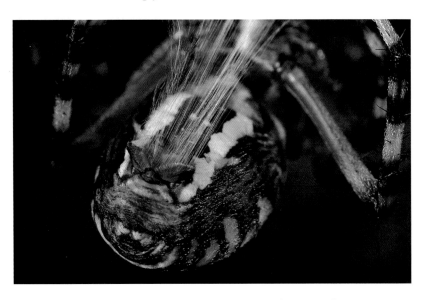

have to wear hydrophobic skates close to eleven miles (eighteen kilometers) long.

In the more mundane world of walking, insects use their six legs, which may appear to be an uselessly complicated technique. Yet in-depth studies using walking robots have demonstrated that this arrangement allows the animal to move forward while maintaining an

excellent balance on its legs. It stands on a tripod formed by the first and third leg on one side and the middle leg on the other, while the three other legs move forward; legs on the alternate side are then moved.

The advantages of an alternating tripod movement so impressed engineers that they based designs for crawling machines on insect locomotion. These designs may one day be used to propel remote-control reconnaissance units for the exploration of other planets.

Examining the individual elements making up an insect is something like leafing through an inventory of discoveries by mad scientists. These include oar-shaped legs in aquatic insects, which have abdomens with respiratory tubes similar to underwater divers; the straw-like proboscis in the butterfly; mandible tongs of beetles; the hypodermic needle proboscis of mosquitoes; knife-sharp legs of praying mantis; and brushes and combs in ants and bees located on their front legs and for cleaning their antennae.

Through evolution, accident, and natural selection, insects have acquired a panoply of accessories that seem custom made. Observing nature for an inventive idea is not entirely new. The great naturalist Réaumur devoted a great part of his life to the study of insect behavior. He observed that wasps make their nests from a mixture of wood fiber and saliva, creating a light, high-quality paper in the process. On November 15, 1719, he read his "History of Wasps" to the public meeting of the Science Academy. "Take the example of the paper-wasp," he'd written. "Let's use wood, not rags,

Argiope spider wrapping a cricket in a bundle of silk.

to make our paper. The stock of old clothes is not growing fast enough to satisfy our constantly growing need for paper." More than one century went by before anyone paid attention to this wise suggestion. Today, pure rag paper has become a rarity at an unaffordable price. The much less expensive recipe developed by wasps has taken over the market.

Not only do insects know how to transform raw material taken from their environment into highly sophisticated finished products, but some of their close cousins, the spiders (both spiders and insects are arthropods, along with centipedes, scorpions, and crustaceans) go even further. They contain within their bodies minuscule textile factories, which produce silk threads that have qualities highly coveted by researchers. This silk has an extraordinary stretching capacity, with double the elasticity of nylon and five times the strength of steel. This magical fiber is just now revealing its secrets, and researchers can foresee the day when it may be produced using genetically modified bacteria. Soon, perhaps, parachute cords and seat belts may be made from a recipe stolen from spiders.

A list of human inventions that have been directly modeled from nature or merely co-opted from devices animals have used for millions of years reveals that our powers of innovation may have been overestimated.

Yet what about the wheel, the one famous example that can save humankind's honor? Now here's an invention designed uniquely by man. Yet if we observe a common dung-beetle at work, another surprise lies in store for us. Start-ing with an unshaped clump of cow or sheep dung, it uses its head as a shovel to flatten the chunk, then its legs to form a virtually perfect sphere. It then rolls its creation along, pushing it backwards by pedaling with its rear legs. The dung-beetle wobbles and zigzags along. Its goal is to move its share of the cake as quickly and as far away from other competitors as possible so that it can bury it in a safe spot and eat in peace.

The dung-beetle did not invent the wheel but certainly came close to it; we will grant it the invention of the ball.

There were many dung-beetles in the steppes of ancient Mesopotamia, which seems to have been the source of this great invention somewhere around the middle of the fourth millennium. Who knows? Perhaps their example was a determining factor in the development of this object that changed the destiny of mankind.

Sacred scarab rolling a ball.

Pirate spider walking on water.

Water strider.*

Water strider capturing a dragonfly.*

Aquatic spider and its "diving bell."*

Argiope spider on its web.

Epeirid spider web.*

Mosquito wing.

Dragonfly on the lookout among the horsetails.*

Flower-loving fly in stationary flight.

A swarm of gnats at the end of summer.*

A ladybug taking off from the tip of a blade of grass.*

A praying mantis in flight.

A grasshopper in flight.*

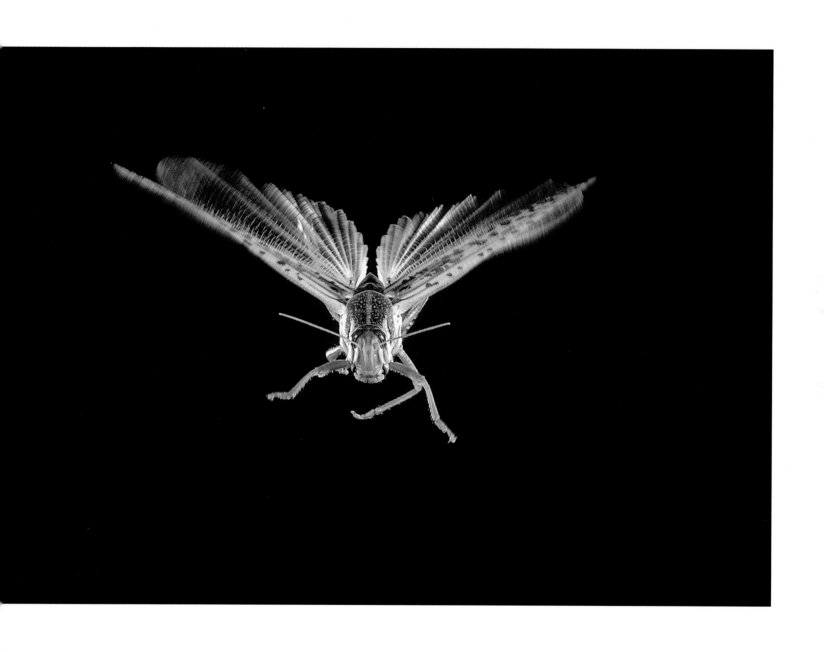

A desert locust at full speed.*

Four seconds in the flight of a fly.*

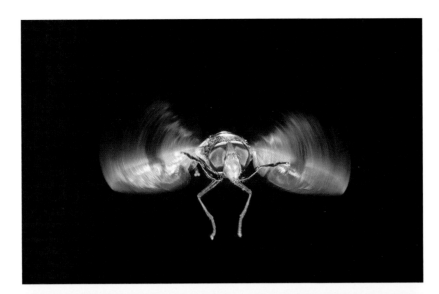

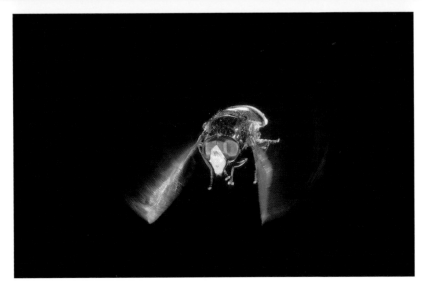

A field of poppies in Provence.

THE PLAY OF INSECT
AND FLOWER

For a scientist, the pleasure of discovery is sometimes a poetic experience. Insect pollination of a flower is part of the special realm of nature where understanding brings a sense of wonderment. The story begins like a fairy tale and includes the secret of the beauty of flowers.

Why are flowers beautiful? We do have an answer to this childlike question. Flowers are beautiful quite simply to seduce insects. They wear exquisite colors, grow into delicate shapes, and unleash sweet scents for insects alone. The insect and the flower share an unusual destiny—a pact agreed upon by an animal and a plant. They are so closely linked that in many cases, one could not survive without the other. Without insects, eighty percent of the flowering plants would disappear from the planet, for lack of descendants.

Flowers need insects in order to reproduce; without their help, most would remain sterile, unable to grow fruit or seeds.

It all started just over 100 million years ago, when the first flowers appeared on Earth. They thrived and pushed out many older plants, such as mosses and ferns. What evolutionary advantage did these newcomers have that produced such a proliferation of insects? The unique aspect of flowers lies entirely in their structure.

A flower is nothing more than a reproductive organ consisting of accessories—the calyx and the corolla—surrounding the male and female elements. The stamen contains the pollen, which are the male seeds that correspond to sperm in animals. The ovary, located in the center of the flower, contains ovules. Above it is a small column, the style; at the end of this are the stigmata. A flower must be pollinated to be fertile, which means that a small amount of pollen must fall on the stigmata. The pollen then germinates and drops down along the long length of the style to join up with the ovule. Given this anatomical configuration, it would appear easy to find ways of fertilizing the hermaphroditic flower. The pollen merely has to move the few millimeters separating it from the stigmata. Yet this direct method

A bee in a poppy.

91

is rarely possible. Self-pollination is outlawed among flowers just as intermarriage is banned between close relatives. Some do attempt this, but their offspring are fragile. They lack the hybrid vigor sought by agronomists. Flowers implement a wealth of precautionary measures to prevent this from occurring. They construct barriers to prevent illegitimate unions. Gentian and epilibium have a time barrier, since the two sexes reach maturity at different periods—the stigmata starts to blossom after the stamen has already wilted. There is a purely material barrier among some orchids, including the vanilla plant, which has a membrane preventing contact between the male and female parts.

The incapacity of the vanilla plant to self-pollinate led to an interesting discovery in the mid-nineteenth century. At that time, the use of vanilla as a flavoring for chocolate presaged a wealthy future for plantation owners. Someone had the idea of expanding vanilla-raising to countries other than its native soil of Mexico. The plant thrived in the tropical climate of the Indian Ocean islands, but with one minor problem: it never produced vanilla beans. The cause of this sterility was traced to a single bee—the Melipona—capable of bypassing the small membrane to pollinate the flower. The problem was that the Melipona lived only in Mexico. Growers had to find another way to obtain the fruit because the insect refused to become acclimatized anywhere but Mexico. A young man in the Reunion Islands came up with the idea of hand-pollinating plants by using a bamboo twig. This system is still widely used today on large vanilla plantations—some 18,000 flowers per day can be fertilized by a single person.

Another reason often prevents self-pollination—some plants are simply sterile to their own pollen.

Unable to ensure the critical step of fertilization on their own, flowers need partners in order to reproduce. But how to contact this partner? Plants are immobile, tied to the ground by their roots. Yet they do have one strategy: to make pollen travel. Some plants, such as the pine tree and larch, rely on the wind for transportation, but this solution involves a tremendous amount of waste. Only a few of the many thousands of seeds produced ever reach their goal. This blind-carrier technique was soon abandoned for an infinitely more efficient method of conveyance.

When an insect lands on a flower to gather nectar, it throws everything in its path into chaos. It moves around in all directions and bumps into the stamen, which unleashes a rain of pollen. Powdered from its antennae to the ends of its legs, the insect continues along its route, visiting other flowers; at each stop the pollen covering its body shakes off as it moves. In the process, some pollen invariably ends up landing on the stigmata. The flower has achieved its goal of cross-pollination—the insect has provided the fertilizing pollen from the stamen of another plant.

Flowers have developed even more extravagant systems to improve the transfer of pollen and insects have learned how to make best use of the miraculous nectar flowers produce. How can anyone question the efficiency of such a mutually beneficial commerce?

On any beautiful spring day, thousands of bees can be seen in flowering orchards and fields. A simple experiment reveals the importance of these bees. If one branch of a pear tree is carefully sealed off for several months, not one of the thirty flowers on the branch will produce a pear. The other branches, however, will be laden with fruit. Fruit-growers know how much the success of their crops is due to the bee population. When a few hives are placed alongside their clover or sainfoin fields, seed and fodder productivity increases almost to one hundred percent. Some four hundred melon seeds must be fertilized for one good, round fruit to develop. But the flower opens only for one day, early in the morning, and closes that same afternoon. Enough bees must therefore be around to ensure the four hundred pollinations, or the fruit will be misshapen and unfit for consumption.

The bee's assiduous activity is proverbial. These zealous nectar-gatherers do not, however, visit meadow flowers by accident. They have definite preferences. They are sometimes attracted by a scent, sometimes by a shape or color. Curiously, the flowers we consider most beautiful are also the ones that attract the most insects. This is mere coincidence—a flower gains nothing from our attention except the chance to end its life in a glass vase. Attracting insects, on the other hand, is vital to the flower.

Flowers have developed an entire range of tricks to seduce insects. The first step is to catch its attention by displaying spectacular colors.

The multicolored corollas are like flags flying in the distance and can be seen by insects flying high over a meadow. Large petals are more successful than smaller ones. Tiny flowers, however, grouped together in large clumps, also manage to make themselves visible. Although the umbels of the wild carrot, the capitulum of the daisy, and the bunches of wisteria and lilacs are all on a single stem, they all form small "bouquets."

Flowers sport a profusion of colors, but it is interesting to note the almost total absence of red in our flora, aside from the poppy, the wild carnation, and a few others. Among insects, only butterflies are able to distinguish this color (bees, for example, are totally blind to red—see Chapter One). In tropical countries, however, scarlet flowers are extremely common; interestingly, they are not pollinated by insects but

The blossoming of a wild rose.

by nectar-loving birds such as the hummingbird or the colibri. These birds extract nectar by remaining in stationary flight like a helicopter over the flowers, drawing the sweet liquid up through their long beaks. Birds have a marked preference for red. This is spectacular proof that the colors of flowers are aimed selectively at the animals—birds or insects—capable of pollinating them.

Floral scents also enter into this seductive campaign. Aside from the lime tree and a few highly scented woods that spread waves of perfume, scent alone is rarely enough to attract an insect in flight. Its effectiveness is limited and is primarily aimed at reviving flagging interest. This is an important role, since nectar-gathering insects often have a highly developed sense of smell. The bee is much more sensitive to floral scents than are humans; through its antennae, a bee perceives scents we do not even know exist. Truly scentless flowers are a minority in nature; they are generally large, brightly colored flowers such as the digitalis, bearbine, colchicum, and tulip. The intensity of the visual signals is such that other techniques of attraction are not necessary.

Floral scents are not only intended to pique an insect's sense of smell. Among bees, odors are also used to transmit important messages. Karl von Frisch's fascinating discoveries concerning the language of bees demonstrate that when a worker has collected a good harvest of nectar, it returns to the hive and performs a particular dance for the other bees. Depending on the choreography the bee has chosen—short wriggles or furious circles—the others learn not only of

the existence of a rich plunder but also its distance and direction from the hive. One final detail removes any risk of confusion: the scent of the dancer. The flower impregnates the bee with an odor that the workers store in their memory as a guide in the field. They instantly recognize the particular species among other flowers of the same color.

Despite their powerful charms, scents and colors would not suffice to ensure a loyal, abundant workforce without one final compelling and irresistible argument: nectar. Nectar is the final reward offered to the pollinators for services performed. The first flowering plants, however, did not provide nectar; they had only pollen. This situation suited certain insects of the period—beetles, for example, whose mouth organs were well designed to grind plant tissue but totally unable to suck up any liquid. By eating the pollen, these primitive beetles became the first messengers for flowers. Beetles today are still closely associated with the most archaic botanical families, such as magnolias. They also visit some of the pollen flowers that have thick stamens but no nectar; these include roses, peonies, and cistus. Plants sometimes pay a high price for the awkwardness of these insects, which may outweigh the benefits they provide. Some goldsmith beetles do not merely graze on the pollen—they indiscriminately break parts of the flower and devour buds. This devastation often causes irreparable damage to the plant.

With the development of the true nectar-gatherers, these rough methods came to an end. The first flowers with nectar—tiny glands located at the base of the petals that secrete a sugary liquid—appeared at the same time. Instruments other than the "shears" of the beetles were required to reach this new beverage. Bees, flies, and butterflies became specialized at this. The cutting mandibles were replaced by delicate, flexible tongues suited to harvesting nectar. Together, insects and flowers took a step forward in the history of evolution.

The shape of corollas also changed over time, with the development of more platformlike flower clusters that made it easier for an insect to land on them. The tubular flowers constructed complicated structures that made them interdependent on their partners. The nectar in daffodils, orchids, and valerian is buried deep within a long corridor and is accessible only to a small number of insects. This tube is so long in certain flowers that it is possible to predict the type of insect capable of penetrating it. In the late nineteenth century, the naturalist Charles Darwin examined a Madagascar orchid in which the nectar was located more than eight inches (twenty centimeters) deep. He was convinced that a butterfly with a spectacularly long tongue had to exist somewhere on the island. Twenty years later, the Macrosilia butterfly was discovered; its proboscis was indeed this length. It was named *predicta* in tribute to Darwin's perspicacity.

Providing nectar is a clever way to attract hungry insects, but to tell them exactly where to find it goes beyond a flower's call of duty. Signs on the petals draw a clear map indicating the path to the nectar, which saves valuable time for both parties. A clearly marked path also

prevents impatient visitors from becoming discouraged. The configuration of the corollas is sometimes extremely complex and changes considerably from one flower to another. These street signs—in the form of variable shapes and colors—all have one thing in common: they form lines that converge on the nectar-producing gland. The scarlet lines on digitalis and the wide striations on veronica, mauve, and iris guide the insect toward the sugary source. The scent on these spots is different and more intense than on the rest of the flower. Some signals, invisible to human eyes, reflect ultraviolet light. Others correspond to specific sectors of the corolla and totally absorb these light rays. To a bee, the petals of a potentilla—which to our eyes appears uniformly yellow—have contrasting dark spots in their centers.

You merely have to watch bees gathering nectar to see how effective the nectar signs are. When a bee lands on a flower for the first time, it takes a long time before discovering the hidden nectar. After the third or fourth attempt, it becomes more agile. If you are patient, you would be astonished to see it drawing out nectar with an almost machinelike precision. Bees carefully select the flowers they visit by limiting themselves to the same species for several days at a time. This saves them a great deal of time, because they don't have to relearn a new location constantly. Who could ask for a better messenger than someone who can deliver his package to the right spot without making any stops or detours? Pollen traveling on the back of a bee increases the chances of fertilization and prevents it from landing on a species of flower on which it could not germinate.

None of these floral attributes exist in plants that use wind to carry their pollen. The flowers of these plants are generally small and odorless and do not have nectar or petals. The pollen of graminaceae, conifers, and catkins, for example, resembles extremely fine, dry dust, which can be carried far and wide by the wind. Among insect-pollinated plants, however, the pollen has large grains, and under a microscope the surface appears to be decorated with delicate sculptures. This is how the pollen adheres so well to the coats of insects during flight.

The best insect pollinators are bees and other hymenoptera. They also have exceptional endurance. In addition to satisfying their individual needs, bees must accumulate enormous reserves of nectar and pollen to feed their larvae. The most evolved flowers allow only the best nectar-gatherers to visit. In extreme cases, the relationship is so exclusive that it is actually dangerous to the flower. Aconite, for example, can be fertilized only by the bumblebee. Its survival depends on this insect alone. Similarly, the high-precision mechanism of the sage plant can be operated only by bees and bumblebees. To remove the nectar, which is located at the base of the corolla, a kind of gate blocking the access must be pushed open. This causes the two long stamens to swing over the bee's back, powdering it with pollen. Although butterflies are excellent nectar-gatherers, they are unable to move this obstacle aside with their slender proboscises.

Bees can manipulate the most sophisticated floral mechanism with dexterity. The alfalfa plant, however, poses a particular problem. It uses a brutal method called "tripping" to deliver its pollen. The stamens violently strike the bee's body just as it spreads apart the petals holding them prisoner. The impact seems to be so unpleasant to the insect that it bypasses the official entry by inserting its tongue sideways, without triggering the tripping mechanism. The alfalfa gains nothing in this case—its nectar is taken, but it receives nothing in exchange. Fortunately, the more corpulent bumblebees are not bothered by the tripping treatment and collect nectar from the alfalfa in the proscribed manner. We have often surprised groups of bees and bumblebees "stealing" nectar. The highly organized bumblebees create an opening on the outside of the tubelike flowers of the balsam and comfrey plant. This direct access to the source of nectar eliminates the necessity of entering the corolla. We can grant certain extenuating circumstances in the theft of nasturtium nectar, since it is concealed at the base of a very long spur. In Peru, where this plant originally came from, only hummingbirds were capable of pollinating it.

Nectar is not the only bait used by plants to lure insects. They also provide other come-ons. The bell-shaped corollas of the belladonna and the campanula, for example, offer an ideal shelter against the rain and wind. In the Amazon, groups of scarabs rush to take refuge for the night in the heart of the giant water lily known as the *Victoria regia*. The flowers open in the evening and close at dawn, imprisoning the insect for the day. Covered with pollen, they escape the following night once again to take shelter in other recently opened corollas.

The yucca plant that lives in the deserts of America provides a safe and comfortable nest for insects to lay eggs. The Pronuba moth even lays its eggs inside the ovaries of the flower. As soon as it blooms, small caterpillars eat the mature seeds lying all around them. This is not, however, a loss for the plant—on the contrary, the reserve of seeds greatly exceeds the caterpillars' needs. Some four-fifths survive unscathed. Furthermore, the seeds are able to mature because of the butterfly's work. Just after mating, the male butterfly collects yucca pollen in its proboscis, which it uses as a pair of hooks to create a small ball. It then flies with this package to a nearby flower. As soon as it arrives, it slips several eggs into the ovary using its ovipositor, which is a sort of planter located

at the tip of its abdomen. Finally, it climbs up to the stigmata to leave its offering: a small portion of the ball of pollen. It repeats this operation from one flower to another until it has entirely used up the pollen. The Pronuba moths do not eat the nectar or the pollen—their interest in pollen reflects an instinctive maternal concern. If the yucca flowers were not fertilized by the butterfly, the seeds would not develop and the caterpillars would starve to death. To the yucca, the care taken in this pollination process certainly compensates for the loss of a few seeds. The very existence of the moth and the yucca depends on this close association.

Among the countless variations of interplay between insect and flower, there is one example of a plant that is fertilized without offering its benefactor anything in exchange. These are the small orchids called the ophrys. The method used by this highly evolved plant is certainly the most successful example in the history of pollination. To achieve its goal, the ophrys "disguises" itself as an insect. This example of mimicry is extremely rare among plants—it is usually animals who imitate plants to evade their enemies. The names of these orchids—fly ophrys, bee ophrys, bumblebee ophrys, hornet ophrys—reflect their similarity to specific insects. Some thirty years ago a Swedish biologist, Professor Kullenberg, discovered that certain male wasps and wild bees looked upon the ophrys as a sexual partner. Studying the fly ophrys, he was surprised to observe the tricks performed by the Gortyes wasp. As soon as it landed, the insect got an erection and attempted to mate by moving the tip of its abdomen frenetically over the hairy surface of the labellum. A meticulous comparison of the plant decoy and the real female was revealing—not only did they both have a similar size, shape, color and bristle location, but the plant's scent was identical to that of the insect.

Each species of ophrys successfully seduces a particular insect. The bumblebee ophrys most often attracts Eucera bees, while the bee ophrys welcomes the awkward assault of the Macrocerae. These irresistible erotic effigies are created much like papier-mâché masks. The labellum is the initial mold—bumps on the simple petal give the illusion of a rounded volume, similar to an abdomen.

The insect does not immediately understand its mistake. As it frolics, it ends up with two small rods attached to its forehead with a sticky sucker; the end of each of these rods has a pollen sac. When the insect flies to another flower, these stalks gradually lean forward and are thus perfectly positioned to contact the stigmata as soon as the insect, drawn to another flower, assaults another ophrys corolla.

Several observers in the early twentieth century described the strange liaison between the hymenoptera and the ophrys. But the story seemed so fantastic at the time that nobody took it seriously.

The evolution of insects and flowering plants has followed two parallel paths for some five million years. Each innovation in the structure of a flower results in a corresponding leap in the insect world, and vice versa. These continuous refinements by both plant and insect have created perfectly matched couples. Today, the equilibrium of the entire biosphere depends on the cooperation between these two protagonists.

A bee gathering the pollen from a wild rose.

A bee inside a lady's-slipper orchid.*

Flies imprisoned in an arum flower.*

A solitary bee attempting to mate with an orchid.*

102

A sphinx moth foraging in a valerian flower.

103

Above:
A bee leaving the corolla of a poppy.

Right:
Poppy flowers.

Above:
A bee activating the "rocking stamen" of a sage plant.*

Left:
A bumblebee entering an iris flower.

107

Above:
A bee flying amid viper's bugloss.

Left:
A bee sucking the nectar from a lavender flower.

Above:
Scotch broom stamens powder the back of a bee.*

Right:
Apollo butterfly on a rhinanthus flower cluster.

110

Above:
A fly ensnared in a butterwort leaf.*
Right:
Butterwort in flower.

114

Above:
Green lacewing imprisoned by a drosera.*

Left:
Leaf of the carnivorous drosera plant.

A Syrphus fly captured by a drosera.

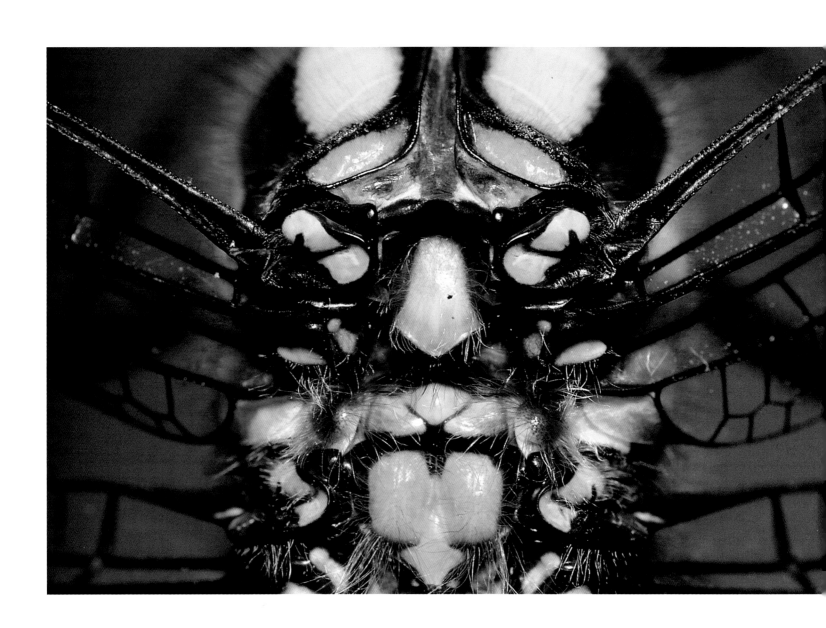

Detail of the thorax of an Aeschna cyanea.

THE ART OF APPEARANCES

There are as many kinds of insects as there are stars in the sky. This multitude exceeds the boundaries of our imagination. The figures put forward are so high they are purely abstract. Entomologists have spent several centuries classifying some one million different insects. The result of this overwhelming task probably gives only a fragmented overview of the wealth of entomological fauna. Unexplored tropical regions are swarming with unknown species. Some scientists estimate that nine-tenths of the world's insects have not yet been discovered. Yet every form of this dizzying profusion has the same basic makeup—six legs, four wings, two antennae—that classifies an animal as an insect. Given the number of combinations, it seems as though nature must have exhausted the range of possibilities and used up all its inventive and adaptive resources.

The phrase "quirk of nature" is often used to describe a collection of exotic insects with multicolored coats and baroque decoration. But the insect, even when it is more splendid than our most precious jewels, cannot be reduced to a mere collector's item. It is a living creature evolving within an environment under the watchful eyes of thousands of other animals. This is where we are likely to find the reasons for its appearance.

An observation of insects in nature shows two distinct options: the flamboyant, provocative costume that attracts the eye and captures our attention, or the camouflage that confers invisibility.

Discretion is the attitude chosen by the largest number of insects. It procures a dual advantage: to escape the eyes of enemies and, if necessary, to be invisible to the desired prey. The coat of the large green grasshopper blends in perfectly with the color of the long meadow grasses in which the insect hides throughout the summer.

This camouflage is not entirely passive; when the animal is worried, it executes an effective ruse. If a grasshopper observes something unexpected, it shifts slightly along the stem supporting its weight to move behind it. If the

The elytra of exotic beetles are covered with colorful scales.

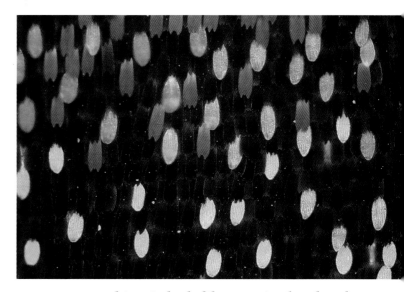

intruder moves around the grass, the insect moves around in the opposite direction, always putting the stem between it and the danger. The insect will turn around the piece of grass several times if you are willing to walk around its perch.

The plant kingdom, or green world, is the background against which an insect evolves throughout its life—indeed, plants often provide them with room and board. It is therefore not surprising that countless insects—crickets, grasshoppers, bugs, and butterflies—are the same color as chlorophyll. An insect's life is ephemeral. For those born in the spring or early summer, green is clearly the color of choice. But species that live through late summer face a problem: plants turn a more tawny color. The truxalis, a small, slender cricket in southern France, solves this problem elegantly by adopting three different outfits in rapid succession. The first, during the adult phase in the middle of the summer, has a light green coat; the second, in late summer, is the yellowish color of dried grasses; and the third, in autumn, is the dark green color that plants turn after a later rain.

It is wise to imitate color, yet it is even better to imitate shape, material and texture. The inchworm is a master of this technique. Its bumpy brown body is a perfect reproduction of a thin branch. Some of the protrusions on its skin look exactly like leaf scars. This worm uses its unique body in a sophisticated way. It clutches a branch with its last pair of suckerlike pads, then turns the front part of its body sideways. A silk thread holds its head to the support, making it look like a twig that has been broken off.

The evidence of this quest for invisibility is unsurpassed in the tropical forest. The accurate details on the insects would confound the most scrupulous designer—they seem to be slavish, maniacal copies of the original plant. The pterochroze of South America, for example, imitates leaves. Its elytrons look like wide green limbs crisscrossed by a main rib and secondary veins. These elements are enough to create the illusion of a perfect copy. Yet this insect has developed even more exquisite refinements: the edges of its wings have multiple indentations, as if the false leaf had been nibbled away by insects. Signs of decay occur frequently in many species—the skin of the "leaf" sometimes has sinuous, lighter-colored lines, as if it had been attacked from the inside by a burrowing larva that left behind excrement indicated by a small, central black spot. In other cases, designs of mildew spots alter the appearance of the false leaf—specialists have even been able to recognize a real species in this fake mildew.

How have insects achieved such a perfect imitation of plants? The mimicry of shapes and

Wing of the Indo-Malayan Papilio hoppo.

122

colors has evolved from generation to generation. It is hereditary and genetic, not the result of a deliberate desire for camouflage. Insect behavior, combined with a certain posture, increases the effectiveness of the imitation. Yet this is not a learned skill—the insect adopts the posture matching its borrowed role because the gesture itself is recorded in the chromosomal memory.

Over geological time, natural selection has certainly favored the insects with the best camouflage, which have been better able to escape predators. Sudden and accidental changes have resulted in unexpected shapes that are sometimes even better equipped than before. The newcomers then replace their doomed predecessors. This explanation involves a certain number of suppositions, but recent observations have removed it from the domain of pure conjecture.

Biologists observing the birch moth—a small moth with pale wings resembling birch bark—were able to see natural selection at work. In the area around Manchester, England, soot from factories had blackened the trunks of the birch

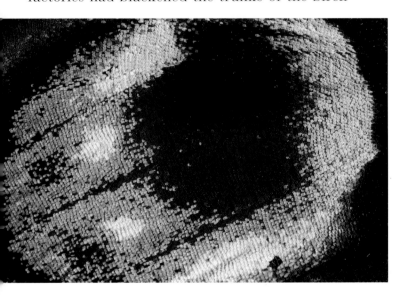

trees; birds, the birch moths' predators, could see them easily as light spots against a dark background. A new, entirely black moth suddenly appeared, a variety rarely seen before since it was poorly suited to its environment. This black moth gradually replaced the original light-colored moths, which were decimated by the birds. This sudden evolutionary change, made necessary by the industrial era, is so unusual that biologists gave it a name that sounds something like a disease: industrial melanism. In some highly industrialized areas of the United States, up to ninety percent of the butterflies are melanic, which does little to brighten up the countryside.

Although we can see that the combined effects of natural selection and mutation have resulted in effective colors and shapes for camouflage, we are stumped by certain extreme cases, such as the pterochroze grasshoppers. It would be just as efficient to imitate a healthy leaf as a sick leaf eaten away on all sides. Scientists sometimes hide their ignorance behind impressive labels. Pterochrozes, for example, are sometimes classified as hypertelic, which means they have developed beyond a useful point.

An insect does not limit itself to passive defense in its efforts to escape its enemies. Camouflage of whatever kind provides only a relative degree of protection. Birds have remarkable visual acuity and can distinguish color much better than humans can—*trompe-l'œil* fools them only partially. Some insects, therefore, suddenly go on the offensive once a predator has broken through their defensive strategy.

Wing scales of the peacock butterfly.

The desired effect is terror. It is essential to strike fast and hard, to disconcert the adversary with a unexpected metamorphosis that will chase it away. The praying mantis is usually a model of discretion. Its all-green coat cannot be seen in the grass, but as soon an overly curious predator comes close, it instantly puts on battle clothes. It raises its elytrons high, fans outs it membranous wings, and twists its front legs in an odd position to the side. It then rubs its abdomen sporadically against its wings to create a strange noise that sounds like crumpling paper. This intimidating demonstration—described by entomologists as a spectral attitude—is sufficiently alarming to drive off the intruder.

This psychological warfare sometimes goes to startling lengths, as with the caterpillar of the puss moth, which spends its life in a willow tree, devouring the leaves as it lies arched upside-down over the branch. It has a fine-grained cuticle and a beautiful light green color. Although well concealed in the foliage, it is sometimes bothered by birds. When this happens, it suddenly swings its body backwards and inflates its thorax, presenting the sight of a bloated grotesque mask. This effigy with a crimson necklace, two spots for eyes, and a large flat nose is actually the caterpillar's real head. To top off this incongruous sight, two bright red coils wrap around its tail in all directions.

This frightening effect can be achieved with simpler methods. Some insects have pushed this economy of mimicry to the extreme—only the eyes remain visible. Indeed, a black mask worn at a ball is not really fearsome; it only appears to be so because it alters facial characteristics. The eye-shaped designs, or eyespots, on butterfly wings, have a more powerful effect because they are removed from any recognizable context. The grand emperor moth has so perfected this technique that its eyespots are perfect imitations of shining eyes. It achieves this effect through a tiny fault in the covering of the wing, which reveals the transparent membrane underneath. The eyespots are often only on the rear wings, and are therefore invisible when the butterfly is at rest. By merely sliding its front wings, the butterfly can suddenly uncover two fake eyes.

Experiments have shown that when the eyespots are removed, many more butterflies are gulped down by birds, who do not like to be stared at. The frozen gaze of the butterfly wings often chases away a potential predator.

We may rarely see the millions of insects camouflaged in the countryside. Yet take a few steps into a meadow and you'll probably come across a brilliantly colored butterfly, caterpillar, or bug. These animals make no attempt to hide themselves; indeed, they remain in plain sight. What to make of this casualness? The zygene butterfly with red and black wings sits tranquilly atop a flower; it flies away indolently as we approach, almost with regret. It is important to know that it contains cyanic acid, a strong poison that makes it inedible. When a bird grabs it in its beak, it quickly spits the butterfly back out; from then on, it looks upon the flashy plumage as a warning sign saying, "Danger, do not eat." Numerous insects are toxic or secrete bad-tasting substances, in this way proclaiming their danger.

The poisonous stingers on wasps and hornets make them difficult to swallow; these insects have yellow and black stripes that are easily identifiable to predators. The protection these stripes provide is so efficient that many perfectly harmless insects have adopted the same colors. Several species of flies, butterflies, beetles, and crickets also have yellow and black stripes. They even imitate the behavior of other insects; Syrphus flies vibrate their wings just like wasps, while Clytus beetles ape their jerky movements.

The reasons for an insect's appearance—to remain invisible, warn, or frighten an enemy through bluff or real danger—results from millennia of natural selection. The best camouflage, the most intimidating masks, and the most visible warning colors were encouraged because the insects with these characteristics were more often saved from their enemies; they were therefore better equipped in their struggle to survive. The appearance of insects developed as a result of the watchful eyes of others.

The world of insects is too vast to remain imprisoned by theories, however ingenious and seductive they may appear. Natural selection implies a tyrannical predominance of the utilitarian in the evolution of living creatures. There would seem to be little room for gratuitous beauty. Yet how many extravagant thoracic sculptures do we see, how many chiseled helmets and multicolored decorations on wings and elytrons for which we can find no functional explanation?

Must we always seek pure efficiency in a realm that encompasses such a bountiful profusion of shapes and colors? Perhaps life can tolerate, or even encourage, structures that are more than merely useful.

In the insect world, we are either subjugated by the beauty of contemplation or seeking an interpretation, a goal that always lies just

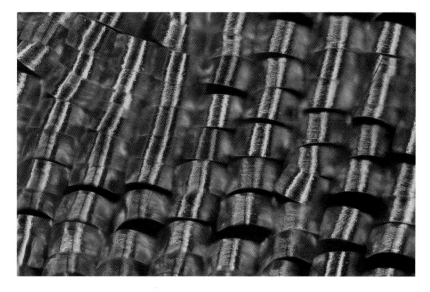

beyond reach. We do not know most of the words of the language spoken by nature, yet we can hear the marvelous sound it makes.

Behind its fearless mask, the insect holds the questions to an enigmatic world.

Iridescent wings of the Urania *butterfly from Madagascar.*

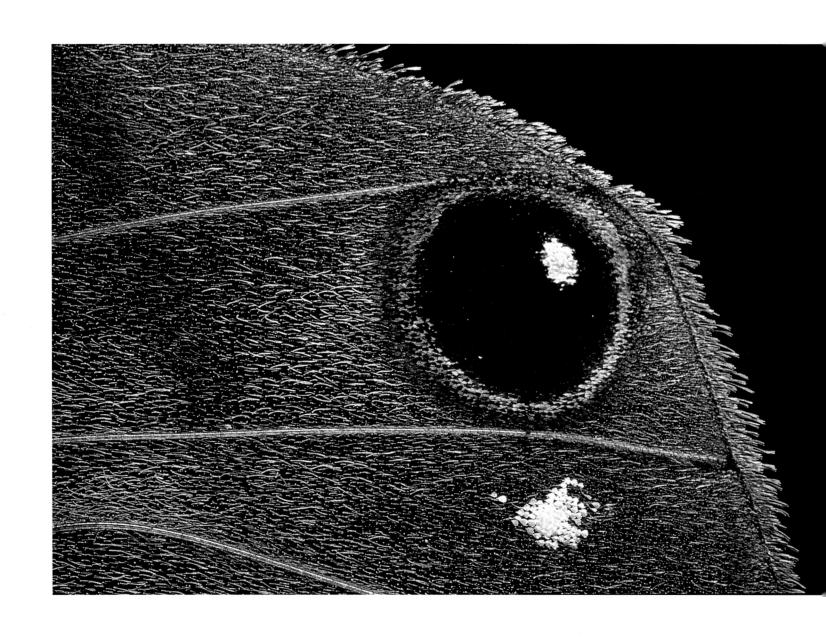

Wing of a *Callitaera piera*. Detail of an eyespot.*

126

Wing of a Cynthia moth.

Above:
Detail of a peacock butterfly wing under a microscope.*
Right:
Two-tailed pasha.

Above:
A ladybug climbing an ear of grain.*

Right:
A ladybug on a head of wheat.

130

Caterpillar of the puss moth in camouflage...*

132

...and in an intimidating stance.*

The comma butterfly.

Mantis from Arabia.*

Above:
Larva of the *Empusa egena* on the branches of a gorse bush.*
Right:
Portrait of an *Empusa egena* larva.*

Above:
Graphosoma italicum under an umbel of parsley.*

Right:
Newly hatched stinkbugs around their eggs.

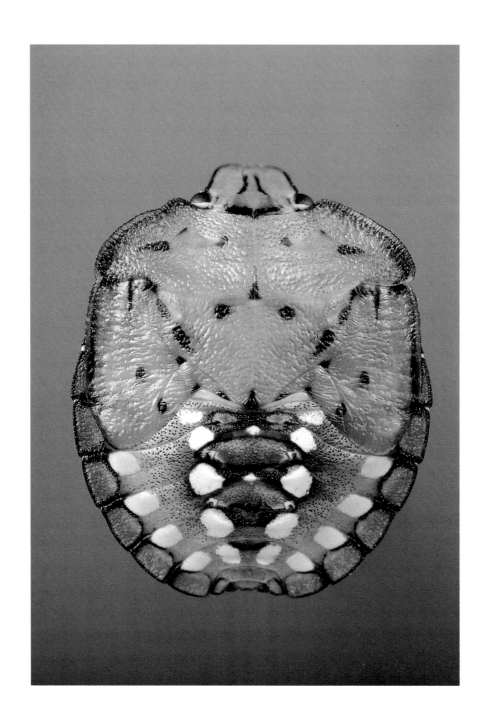

Above:
A field bug.*

Right:
Cercopis vulnerata, a close relative of the cicada, on a stem of dill.

141

Above:
Caterpillar of the owlet moth eating a Scotch broom flower.*

Right:
A praying mantis in "spectral" position.*

A stag beetle.*

A fire wasp playing dead.

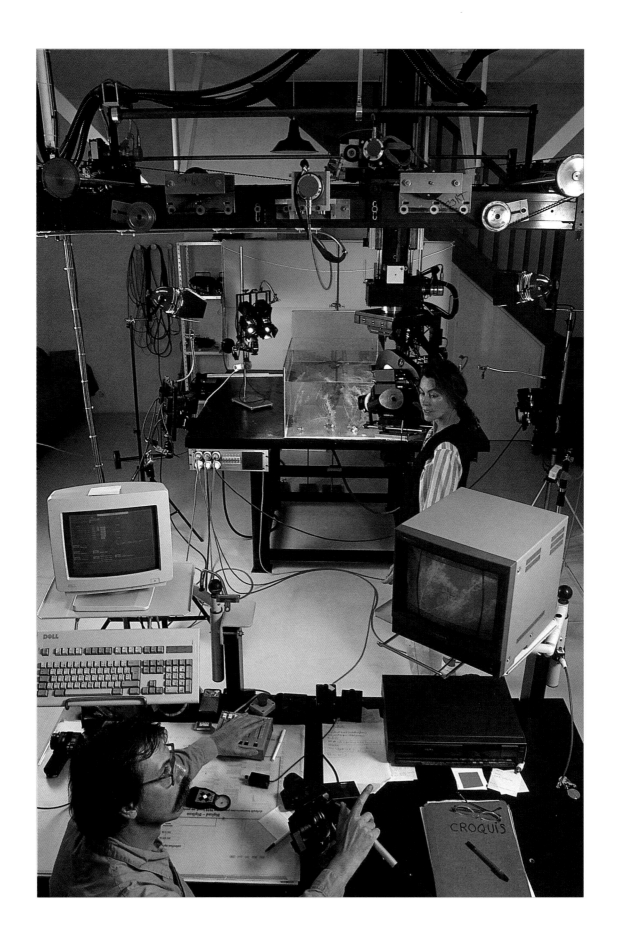

Field studio with filming robot.

CREATION OF A FILM

A film goes through many lives and passes through several metamorphoses from its conception to the moment it appears on the screen. To use the terminology of the insect world, we would say that it is generally happier in its larval stage. This is a time of intense gathering (like a caterpillar's), when we made honey from every good idea we found, a euphoric time when our thoughts could fly free without hitting the hard wall of reality. Filming is a time of stress and permanent crisis, with constant reassessments dictated by unexpected obstacles (and when a film uses insects as stars, the unexpected is the rule). It is an intense, exciting period, when everything is forgotten in a constant struggle against time.

The film lives its final metamorphosis during editing. This is perhaps the most harmonious period in the production of a film because it represents the perfect balance between constraint (the film must be created from a limited number of images) and freedom (several different films can be made from the same rushes).

A CUSTOM-DESIGNED TEAM

We must admit that our early euphoria was short-lived. In a film that requires an unprecedented technical infrastructure, it is hard to develop a scenario without knowing if a practical solution exists to all the possible problems. The tools of professional filmmaking were not created for filming insects.

Right from the start of the project, we decided to break away from the traditional approach used in animal documentary films; we wanted to forget the animal as an object of study moving around in

Waiting for good light to film the poppies.

front of a quasi-immobile camera riveted to a tripod. The idea was to let insects have real roles, like actors in a fictional film. This meant that we had to be able to film with a tremendous freedom of movement, to follow their movements and gestures using pans, long shots, boom shots, and dolly shots, and perhaps combinations of two or more. This was easy to imagine but much harder to execute, since the machine capable of these feats had not yet been invented.

Fortunately, when any project begins, an overwhelming optimism blinds the creators to the perils that lie ahead. Otherwise, many an idea would die on the vine, suffocated in a tangle of potential obstacles. The macrocinematographic robot we dreamed of had a difficult birth. It used up the patience and ingenuity of several teams, not to mention the goodwill of the countless specialists who made house calls.

After eighteen months of struggle and doubts, the odd creature was finally ready for action. It was moved into an "open-field" studio constructed specially in a wild region of the Aveyron in France. There it performed its duties without too many problems during the three years of filming. Suspended from the roof, this 660-pound (300-kilo) beast—a very heavy machine to film such light actors— guided our large 35 mm camera perfectly. We were thus able to film at an "insect level" with the flexibility of a hand-held camera and the accuracy of a microscope.

The Grandeur and Misery of Macrocinema

Making a film in which the main characters are insects involves problems other than camera movements. Taking shots at this scale involves a string of constraints that are unique to macrocinema, an inelegant term for an incredibly rich world of observation. Macrocinema means filming objects close up. This term therefore defines a field of cinema according to a technical criteria—the very small distance separating the subject from the camera. Would a filmmaker who was fascinated with faces ever say that he makes "close-up" films? Yet the person who intimately observes small creatures must resign himself to saying, "I do macrocinema."

The film team at the edge of a pond.

148

Macrocinema is more than just a technique; it is an entire approach, a way of seeing the world. The macrofilmmaker is necessarily near-sighted and sees entire worlds in a simple clump of grass. He is a dreamer who must nevertheless process great quantities of technical knowledge to give life to his dreams. The main technical obstacle encountered is depth of field. This is the area that remains in focus in front of and beyond the focal point of the camera. In close-up filmmaking, this depth is independent of the focal length of the lens used. It depends instead on the aperture of the lens as well as on the reproduction ratio R (which indicates the ratio between the size of the image on the screen and the size of the filmed subject). With a 1/4-inch-long ant, R = 1 if the image of this ant is also 1/4-inch long on the film (which, projected on a twenty-six-foot [eight-meter] screen, shows the audience an ant close to thirteen feet [four meters] long).

For a given opening, the depth of field decreases as R increases. If the value of R remains the same, the depth of field increases as the diaphragm is stepped down. When R = 1 and the diaphragm is set to an aperture of f16, the depth of field is less than one-eighth of an inch. Filmed from the front, only the head of our ant would be in focus, while the top of its abdomen would be totally out of focus. It we move even closer to our subject, for a value of R = 4, the depth of field drops to one-sixteenth of an inch; nothing but the eyes of the ant are in focus.

There is only one way to offset this striking loss of depth of field, and it is extremely limiting; it requires closing down the diaphragm of the lens. And this technique has other drawbacks: the image definition can be altered because of the diffraction that occurs with smaller apertures. In practice, for a ratio of R = 1, it is better to keep a setting of f22 or even f16 (indeed, the diaphragm scale of many lens does not goes higher than f16); for a higher ratio, an aperture setting of f16 or f11 is required.

In Quest of Light

An abundant supply of light is necessary when the smallest lens opening is used. Macrocinema's incessant demand for light is exacerbated by something called the length of focus.

Radio-controlled helicopter carrying a miniature 35mm camera for filming a shot of a dragonfly in flight (Moving Cam technique).

When the focusing ring on the lens in turned from infinity to the closest possible distance, the entire optical unit moves forward, away from the film plane. This movement corresponds to the length of focus. For very close-up views, a large length of focus is necessary, which considerably decreases the luminosity of the lens. When R = 1 for a given diaphragm setting and light reading, four times less light falls on the film than when the lens is focused at infinity. This loss can be offset by opening the diaphragm by two stops—which reduces the depth of field, an essential parameter in macrocinema—or by increasing the amount of light if artificial lighting is available. Therefore, when R = 1, with a lens setting of f16, you would need as much light as if the lens was set to f32 but focused at a normal distance. Using the sensitive movie film available today, which has an ISO rating of 500, you would still need close to twice the light shining from the midday sun in summer.

Macrofilmmakers constantly came up against this light barrier. What the sun is unable to illuminate must be lit artificially. Yet flooding insect actors with light was not a solution if we wanted to keep them comfortable and film their everyday activities accurately.

The use of heat filters removes the infrared spectrum, resulting in a "cold" light. The actors are then free to interpret their natural roles without being disturbed by a stressful environment.

During filming, the lens was often no more than a few inches from the insect or even a few quarter-inches when we filmed a close-up of its face. Yet most insects did not seem to consider this enormous glass eye pointing at it as a threatening presence. Indeed, a curious insect would sometimes penetrate into the lens mount, which lay within its grasp. This is one of the calculated risks of filming unusually small actors.

A Studio in the Field

The need to use intense light sources as well as the guidance system for a high-tech camera motivated our decision to film some of the segments in a studio. But this was a field studio, something like a waiting room in nature. All we had to do was push open the doors to be in the midst of wild grasses

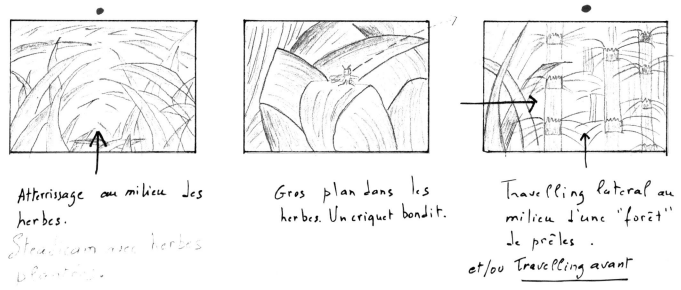

Detail of the storyboard: the start of the film.

and surrounded by clouds of butterflies and bees, all of them drawn to a veritable garden of paradise consisting of buddleias (still known as "butterfly trees"), elders, robinia, lavender, valerian, and sage.

Another essential condition to achieve the interpenetration between studio shots and those filmed outdoors (both kinds of shots feature in most of the film sequences) was to have the studio located in the midst of a protected natural environment. For the most part, the insect actors that appear in the film live in the vicinity of the studio. For the scenes filmed on this site, the insects were moved no more than a few yards, and after filming they were released back into their habitat. The plants were merely borrowed from the nearby fields, so that the plant and flowers are identical in scenes filmed inside and well as out. We therefore had a complete slice of nature in our studio under the glare of our spotlights.

THE ACTORS

If we had conceived of a feature-length film about insects without first developing a detailed scenario, we would have run the risk of creating a sort of super animal documentary, an accumulation of activities selected for their spectacular or aesthetic qualities but not integrated in a continuous narrative. The principle of unity of time and space was quickly adopted. *Microcosmos* takes place in a single beautiful summer day, in a field in the Aveyron countryside, on the same site as our home and our film studio. We are familiar with every corner and hiding place in this terrain.

We made our casting decisions according to criteria of character. Too many films have already shown insects as small bloodthirsty robots, tearing each other apart in an endless carnage. We wanted to reinstate them, to reveal their strange beauty and talents, and to place them within the context of their daily lives by demonstrating the fundamental identity of destiny that links all living creatures, even ones as dissimilar as insects and humans.

Showing the problems encountered by the actors in *Microcosmos*—such as the sacred scarab struggling to move its ball of dung backwards over treacherous slopes—creates a link between it and the viewer. These small touches of humor are valuable because they create a sense of intimacy—if we smile

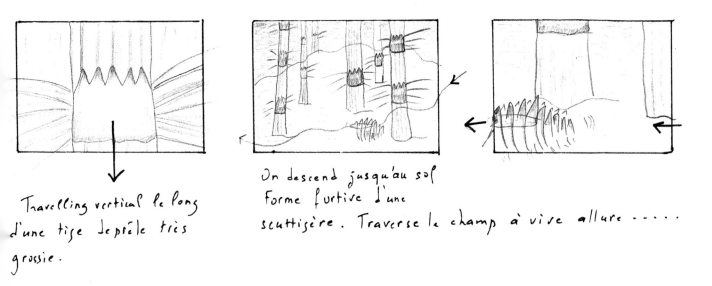

Travelling vertical le long
d'une tige de prèle très
grossie.

On descend jusqu'au sol
Forme furtive d'une
scuttisère. Traverse le champ à vive allure ·····

at the problems of these tiny beasts, is it not because they remind us of some of our own problems? Indeed, this discovery can totally alter our way of looking at them.

This identification, fleeting as it may be, between the viewer and the actors in the film led us to select insects from the countless species living in our region that had some charisma, such as ladybugs, butterflies, dragonflies, and grasshoppers. Others were selected because their activities are similar to our own, such as the sacred scarab and the ant. We also filmed more disturbing characters—water spiders, argiope spiders, and kite beetles—as we did not want to ignore the tragic element of this world (indeed, the dramatic balance of the story would have suffered had we shown only the positive side). Simply put, we wanted to place the violence in context and deal with it in a straightforward way.

In the often risky business of directing our actors, we often observed that several insects from the same species fulfilled the roles in which we cast them with differing levels of success.

Only one of the sacred scarabs we collected was able to roll its ball and bury it while the cameras were turning. The others stubbornly refused to reveal their knowledge in front of witnesses. When, using a very high-speed camera (500 images per second, or twenty times the normal speed) we wanted to film a ladybird taking off from a blade of grass, we quickly found our champion from a stable of some fifty candidates. She took off on cue for almost every take, unperturbed by the powerful spotlights required for the shot.

We are probably inclined to view insects of the same species as interchangeable because of their small size and seemingly identical appearance. Yet, like us, they are individuals and each one is unique in its own way. Once again, we share a common ground.

Filming with a boom.
A continuous zoom from the overall landscape down to the grass.

FILM CREDITS

Directors: Claude NURIDSANY
and Marie PÉRENNOU

Photography: Claude NURIDSANY
Marie PÉRENNOU
Hughes RYFFEL
Thierry MACHADO

Film Editors: Marie-Josèphe YOYOTTE
Florence RICARD

Sound: Philippe BARBEAU
Bernard LEROUX

Original sound: Laurent QUAGLIO

Music: Bruno COULAIS

Executice Producers: Michel FAURÉ
Philippe GAUTIER
Patrick LANCELOT
André LAZARE

Associate Producers: GALATÉE FILMS
Jacques PERRIN
Yvette MALLET
Christophe BARRATIER

Creation and production of the robot
camera: Romano PRADA (Delta Image),
Philippe ROMANO, Bernard RICON (Alten
Industrie).

17 Certain species of solitary bees, such as these longhorn *Eucerae* show the initial signs of social behavior. Each one attends to its own business, but by nightfall, all the males gather together in a shared "dormitory."

18 This long-limbed *Oedemera nobilis* (under 1/2-inch long) spends most of its life inside flower petals, where it gathers pollen. The magnificent iridescent-green coloring is not due to pigment, but to the microscopic structure of the cuticle, which creates interfering light waves, much like the shiny reflections of soap bubbles.

21 The feathery structure on the antennae of giant emperor moths presents a large surface to the surrounding air. They are actually molecule traps that can detect infinitesimal amounts of the female scent. This capacity for "long-distance" seduction (up to several miles) is essential to emperor moths—the females are relatively inactive and the males have a short life span. This sense therefore increases their chances of meeting up.

22-23 The praying mantis is meticulous about cleaning its grasping forelegs and covers every inch methodically. These legs are transformed into spiny sharp knives that grasp and immobilize its prey. At rest, the curved "blade" fits inside the spine-studded groove hollowed out of a "handle." At the approach of a prey, this apparatus unfolds in 1/20th of a second.

24 The sensory world of the ephippiger (wingless grasshopper) is dominated by sound. Its wings have evolved into hornlike stumps unsuitable for flying, but perfect for chirping. A social hierarchy exists among ephippigers living in the same thicket: the leader breaks the silence first, then the others members of the group—always in the same order—join in for a shorter period.

26 These primitive insects have an extremely short life span as an adult—from a few hours to a maximum of several days. However, the aquatic larvae, or nymphs, can live for up to three years.

29 The eyes of a damselfly form two enormous domes that almost cover its entire head. Dragonflies and damselflies are to the insect world what eagles are among birds. These great hunters spot their prey in flight and swoop down, to gather it between their claws.

32 Harvester ants are specialists at gathering seeds. In single file, they carry their loot along two-way "avenues"—some return to the nest, while others go back for more seeds. The seeds are stored for several months in underground "storerooms" before they are eaten.

34 These two desert locusts in the last molting stage (the insect on the right shows well-developed wing parts), sport a jewel-like coloring. With this easily identified "uniform," the many desert locusts traveling through the desert can recognize each other, thereby increasing the cohesion of the group.

37 The gadfly's metallic eye color is due to interfering light waves reflecting off the countless corneas of the compound eye (a similar phenomenon occurs in soap bubbles and pools of oil).

38 The two retractable claws on the leg are used for steep terrain. The fleshy pad, or pulvillus, covered with thousands of flattened bristles, is wonderful for walking across glass windows and ceilings—the minute spatulas adhere to a support through the simple effect of molecular attraction.

39 Fly eyes—framed by a pair of short antennae—have up to 4,000 facets. The enormous trunklike mouthpart, an articulated arm that emerges from under its head, branches into two spongy lobes filled with tiny passages. It can only suck up food in liquid form.

48-49 Crickets—like bugs, cicadas, mantises, and dragonflies—undergo an incomplete metamorphosis: their larvae share a certain number of characteristics with adults and the wings develop more fully with each molt. During the imaginal or final molt, the larva metamorphoses into an adult. The cricket's head and thorax emerge first through a split along the back of its carapace, followed by the abdomen and the hind jumping legs. At first, the wings are short and crumpled; they soon unfold as blood is pumped into the veins.

54-55 Paper wasps construct their nests in the spring; they are started by a single wasp, the queen. She lays an egg at the base of each cell, from which a pudgy larva is born, and she feeds them with prechewed caterpillars and flies. When the larva has completed its growth, it blocks off the cell with a convex cover. After several days, it has metamorphosed into a perfect insect; it uses its mandibles to cuts through the cover and discovers the world through its sensitive antennae.

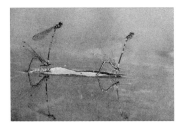

56-57 As they mate, these two partners fly in a pattern that resembles an upside-down heart. The male—on top—clasps the female just behind the head using a claw located at the tip of its abdomen. The female curves her body upward to collect her partner's seed. Once fertilized, the female uses her body to find plants on the water's surface where she can lay her eggs. The male remains coupled to the female while she deposits her eggs.

60 For flies, the pupa is the equivalent of the chrysalis for a butterfly. The body of the maggot dissolves within the brown pupa through a process of autodigestion. The shape of the future insect forms slowly from this living pulp. To break out of its prison, the young fly uses an inflatable device—it contracts its abdominal muscles to send blood to a bulge projecting from its head; this bulge then expands like a balloon. It extricates itself from its case and slowly unfolds its wings. Thirty minutes later, it is ready to fly and conquer the world.

73-74 The oily bristles lining the ends of the water-strider's legs allows it to move fearlessly across the water's surface, its hunting grounds, without getting wet. When an insect—such as this dragonfly—accidentally falls in the water, sensory organs in the strider's legs pinpoint the exact location of the prey from the concentric waves it creates as it struggles in the water.

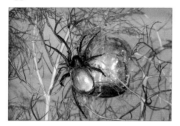

75 The aquatic spider constructs its web in the shape of a diving bell in the midst of aquatic plants. It then captures large bubbles of air between its hind legs and fills the web with air. It then stays dry—under water. The modern underwater homes that allow scientists to work under the surface of the ocean were designed according to a similar principle.

77 A spider's silk thread is secreted from the tip of its abdomen by one to three pairs of tiny spinnerets, which are riddled with holes. The silk is produced by silk-glands that rival the complexity of industrial chemical plants. This silk is actually a cord formed of several dozen individual strands woven together. Depending on the final use, the spider can modify the components of the silk, just as textile manufacturers combine different types of fibers.

79 A broad-bodied dragonfly watches over its hunting territory from the top of a horsetail. Equipped with excellent vision, dragonflies catch mosquitoes and mayflies in the air by flying at full speed just above the surface of the water. They hold the speed record for insect flight at approximately 30 mph.

81 In late summer, on a sunny day following a rainy period, compact swarms of thousands of gnats swirl slowly in the air. These aerial clouds consist primarily of males. If a female flies near one of these dancing groups, she is immediately captured by the males as part of a nuptial ritual in which the perception of sounds, scents, and reactions to movement play a predominant role.

82-83 Flight of a ladybug. As it reach the end of a blade of grass, it opens the cover of its lacquered elytra, unfolds its membranous wings and pirouettes backwards. During flight, the elytra act as fixed-bearing surfaces, comparable to airplane wings. It is basically the rear wings that propel the insect in flight. This system, unique to beetles, does not appear to be successful from the looks of the perilous, lurching flight patterns of these armored insects.

85-87 Grasshoppers always fly in a straight line—their flight is merely an extension of their jumps and therefore of short duration. At rest, the rear membranous wings are folded fanlike under the long, narrow, and rigid fore wings for protection. Desert locusts are much stronger. Their wings beat twenty times per second and they can fly up to twenty hours at a stretch. Their maneuvering skills, however, are weak—they fly in straight lines at an almost constant speed.

88-89 The fly has the best flying technique of all the animals. It can perform amazing acrobatic feats. The wings move in an extremely complicated way, operating something like the rotor blade of a helicopter. During an upstroke, the joints position the wings vertically, with the leading edge toward the top. During a downstroke, on the other hand, the wings beat horizontally to provide better lift in flight. The beating wings describe a figure-eight pattern.

100 Because this European orchid resembles majestic tropical species in size and appearance, it is often overpicked in nature. The color of the slipper-shaped lip attracts pollinating insects. The twisted shape of the flower forces the insect to follow a specific path; in so doing, it has to brush up against the reproductive organs as it leaves, ensuring the flower's reproduction.

101 A cut in the pale green spathe, or hoodlike leaf, of an arum reveals—for a brief moment—a swarm of small Psychoda flies imprisoned by the flower. Drawn by the plant's foul scent, they push their way through a thick ring of yellow bristles guarding the entry, in order to reach the base of the spathe. Once past this obstacle, they become hostages: the downward-pointing bristles block their return. After one or two days, the pollen is mature and rains down over the flies. The bristles then wilt, leaving the path clear for the flies, who escape, only to succumb to the scent of another arum plant.

102 The shape, color, hair, and even the scent of the flower of the European *Ophrys* (or bee orchids) bears a striking resemblance to a specific species of solitary bee, the longhorn *Eucera*. The appearance is so deceptive that males of this species take the flowers for female bees and attempt to mate with them! The orchids, which has no nectar, uses this ruse to attract the insect—the bee then receives two small, yellow pollen sacks, which are attached to its forehead by two suction devices.

107 Only highly evolved insects, such as bees and bumblebees, can operate the sophisticated mechanism developed by the sage plant to filter its visitors. To reach the nectar, the insect must use its head to push a gatelike device located at the base of the corolla. This action causes the two long stamen to drop down, thereby covering the back of the bee with pollen. Fertilization occurs when the bee flies to another sage corolla—it drops a few grains of pollen on the pistil, the female organ of the flower.

110 To collect the pollen from the Scotch broom flower, the bee must break two fused petals enclosing the stamen. Freed by the legs of the insects, these stamen burst forth like springs from a watch, scattering a fine layer of pollen over the bee's back and abdomen.

112 They do not metamorphose into butterflies, but instead produce sawflies, a distant relative of wasps and bees. Like true caterpillars, the sawfly larvae are obsessed by a single activity: eating. The colony makes headway by moving its front line from the tip to the base of a leaf, sparing the indigestible ribs.

114 A fruit fly stuck to a butterwort leaf. The trap of the butterwort—a small carnivorous plant that grows in damp climates—functions like flypaper. Dozens of insects get stuck on the leaf clusters, or rosettes, that grow along the ground. The sticky coating on the surface of the limb is secreted by thousands of minute glands. The strange structure of these spindle-shaped glands is visible in this enlargement (magnified 40 times).

117 The role of the assailant the insect-plant relationship does not always fall to a member of the animal kingdom. The carnivorous plants take revenge by tricking insects into their lair, where they are captured and eaten. The drosera, for example, which grows in peat bogs in temperate climates, secretes small drops of a sticky substance resembling nectar from the end of its tentacles. Drawn by this promising offer, insects are caught as soon as they land on the leaf and are digested over a period of two to three days. A single drosera plant devours an estimated 2,000 insects during the summer.

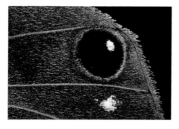

126 Butterflies rely on wing patterns known as eyespots, which resemble wide-open eyes. A slight wing movement brings them suddenly into view, terrorizing the butterfly's attacker. The sparkling effect produced by the *Callitaera piera* is due to a few white scales within the eyespots.

128 A peacock butterfly wing magnified 200 times. Butterfly wings are like living frescoes. The decorative patterns are created by small pigment-filled sacks, or scales, along the wing. A short stem attaches each one to a fold in the transparent membrane of the wing.

130 The familiar red and black-spotted attire of the ladybug is actually meant to be a signal reminding predators that it has an unpalatable taste and is better left alone.

132-133 The caterpillar of the puss moth has two distinct faces. Its green coat is a perfect camouflage when it lies among the willow leaves, its main food source. When a bird arrives and discovers the ruse, the caterpillar rises up and displays a clownish mask by puffing up the front of its thorax, while waving the two red coils around its cleaved tail in all directions. The predator, surprised by this strange sight, flies off.

135 A series of light and dark horizontal lines the same color as the surrounding landscape allow this mantis from Arabia to disappear into the bushes. Military camouflage uniforms use the same principle of random spots and mottling–the form appears as disparate elements that blend into the background.

136 The larva of the *Empusa* lives unseen among the branches of bushes, carefully balancing on its long stilt-like legs; Few people ever catch a glimpse of its gangling form–it sits unmoving, like a twisted twig, an anonymous shape among the tangle of dried plants.

137 This strange face, crowned with two gazellelike horns and an extravagant flattened miter–attributes worthy of a priest's flamboyant attire–belongs to a small insect in southern France called the *diablotin*. It is the larva of the *Empusa*, a close relative of the praying mantis. We don't know the purpose of this headdress, which looks like a decorative whimsy of nature.

138 This *Graphosoma italicum* sits in plain sight, without fear, sucking the sap from umbels. Its striped coat protects it from birds. These bugs can often been found on parsley or wild carrot, known as Queen Anne's lace. The plants reinforce the protective coloring of the bug, and contribute to a stronger concentration of its particularly disagreeable odor.

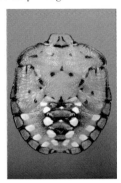

140 In defense, bugs emit clinging, repulsive odors from special glands located under their thoraxes. Some combine this tactic with "warning colors." Others use camouflage, such as this bug belonging to the *Brachynema* family–its predominantly green coat blends in with the meadow grasses.

142 The caterpillar of this emperor moth lives among Scotch broom flowers, its exclusive food. The color of its coat makes it hard to see in the midst of the brilliant yellow of the flower-covered branches.

143 When worried, the praying mantis offers a spectacular demonstration of intimidation. Planted on its hind legs, with all its wings unfolded, abdomen arched and trembling all over, it spreads its grasping forelegs apart, revealing two black-lined spots, called eyespots, which terrorize the predator.

144 This beetle has enormous mandibles with toothed jaws that resemble deer horns, which explains their name, the stag beetles. In combats between males, these are more intimidating than effective–these "stags" are essentially dissuasive weapons.

Designed by Benoît Nacci

Photographs from « Creation of a film »
Page 146 (Éric Teyssèdre) – Page 149 (Renaud Dengreville)
Pages 147, 148 and 153 (Gilles Tordjeman)

Copyright © 1996
Éditions de La Martinière, Paris (France)

Published in 1997 by
Stewart, Tabori & Chang,
a division of U.S. Media Holdings, Inc.
575 Broadway
New York, NY 10012

Distributed in Canada by
General Publishing Co. Ltd.
30 Lesmill Road, Don Mills
Ontario, Canada M3B 2T6

Distributed in Australia and New Zealand by
Peribo Pty Ltd.
58 Beaumont Road
Mount Kuring-gai
NSW 2080, Australia

Distributed in all other territories (except South Africa) by
Grantham Book Services Ltd.
Isaac Newton Way
Alma Park Industrial Estate
Grantham, Lincolnshire
NG31 9SD England

Library of Congress Catalog Card Number: 96-70864

ISBN: I-55670-555-7

Printed in France